CREDIT SPREAD OPTIONS FOR BEGINNERS 2021

Crash Course to find out how to trade with the credit spread

CONTENTS

INTRODUCTION

As the stock market continues its improbable rise from the lows caused by the pandemic earlier in 2020, a new retail trading phenomenon is taking hold. Thanks to the creation of zero commissions and zero fee options trading, everyone with a Robinhood account seems to be buying out of the money (OTM) call options on stocks and profiting massively. The tech stock driven rally fueled this boom, and suddenly, everyone was "trading" options successfully.

As with stocks, it's easy to make money with options in a market that goes up all the time. However, when the tides turn, it turns out that just writing calls on momentum stocks doesn't work so well. We witnessed this in September 2020 when companies such as Tesla and Apple that had been going up without any end in sight, suddenly began going the other way. Resulting in many investors left holding onto worthless OTM calls.

In an ideal world, you'd always face one of the following two scenarios.

1. You buy a stock (or buy a call option), and the price immediately skyrockets.
2. You short a stock (or buy a put option), and the price immediately plummets.

However, in the real world, stock prices don't work like this. In fact, they don't experience too many strong trending moves. While it's easy to point at the previous decade and say that the markets have been rising all the time, this rise was punctuated by long stretches of sideways movements.

The kind of exponential rise that most novice investors expect rarely happens in reality. For the most part, around 80-85% of the time, markets tend to move sideways or slightly upwards. This lack of movement makes directional trading extremely difficult.

Both long-term investors and more active traders can find these sideways periods boring. For investors, the fear of missing out sets in as you see stocks you don't own rising in price, while the ones you do own remain flat. For traders, these periods are when they shoot themselves in the foot because of their compulsive need to do *something*. Being an active trader requires you to participate in all market conditions, and this automatically means making consistent profits is a lot harder. Most active traders resent sideways moves since these moves make it impossible to profit from price differences. You can't buy low and sell high (or vice versa) in a sideways market, after all.

HOW TO WIN CONSISTENTLY

Active traders have a problem with sideways markets because their default approach is to try and predict the market's direction. This means they spend their time looking for directional cues and use all the tools at their disposal to figure out the short-term direction of the instrument they're trading. When presented with the fact that the markets move sideways, for the most part, they simply shrug and look at sideways markets as obstacles to be overcome.

We contend that if the markets are sideways-bound for the most part, surely it makes more sense to use *non-directional* trading strategies. After all, why should you attempt to swim against the tide when you can make money swimming with it.

Every investor and trader's wish is to generate more consistency in their results. A secondary wish might be to show screenshots of 2,000% gains to their family and friends. We're sorry to say, none of the strategies inside this book will net you 2,000% on a single trade. Instead, this book will help you generate consistent returns month after month while not losing sleep over your positions. In our opinion, that's the acid test that every strategy has to fulfill. This means, whether you're an investor looking to generate additional income from your portfolio, or a directional trader looking for strategies to employ in a sideways market, you're in the right place.

It's fully possible to build a non-directional trading strategy that generates reliable profits using options. That is our aim with this book. You don't need to learn a ton of complicated chart patterns or 100 different indicators to make the strategy presented in this book work. *Credit spreads* might sound like a complicated name for a strategy, but once you understand how they work and how they can be best structured, you can implement them in no time at all.

BEING ALMOST CORRECT IS EASIER THAN BEING EXACTLY CORRECT

The core reason these strategies work well is that it's far easier to guess a price range than guess a specific price that a stock will rise/fall to.

Think of it this way. If someone were to ask you what a Rolls Royce Phantom costs, would you be able to guess the price correctly, down to the last cent? Unless you happen to be mad about luxury cars, probably not. However, you can think of an approximate price range quite easily. Even if you only have a cursory knowledge of cars, just the Rolls Royce brand alone is a good indicator. So you could guess that this particular model of car cost "around" half a million dollars.*[1]

What if you could make money guessing stock prices in such approximations? That's the essence of building credit spreads. You can build spreads to take advantage of any market condition, even highly bullish and bearish ones. However, one of the main benefits is that credit spreads also work well in sideways markets. As the markets move sideways most of the time, these strategies will help you take advantage of them.

Many investors want to generate reliable income every month using simple strategies. We will present simple strategies later in this book, which anyone with a basic knowledge of options and the markets can use.

When we say "basic knowledge" we mean that you don't need to understand the specifics of Option Greeks or know 200 different chart patterns. But you will need to know what a call option is and how it's different from a put option.

But don't worry. We will immediately define any new terminology that we introduce throughout this book. So we hope that generating steady and even boring returns is far more appealing to you than generating rockstar-like returns punctuated by severe drawdowns. If a stable, consistent monthly income is what you're after, you've come to the right place.

Once you make these simple strategies a part of your overall investing skillset, you'll realize that you probably won't need many other options trading strategies.

------

1 *For those of you who are into specifics, the base price of the 2020 Rolls Royce Phantom is $457,750

WHY SELLING OPTIONS THROUGH CREDIT SPREADS IS THE BEST APPROACH

I f you've traded options before, you probably remember the first time you bought them. We emphasize the word "bought" because this is the typical way in which novice investors use options. Their affinity for buying options is a holdover from the way they think about the stock market. In stocks, buying comes more naturally than selling.

On the surface, shorting a stock seems a lot less complicated than shorting or writing an option. When you short a stock, you're betting on its price to decrease, and you wait for it to hit lower price levels. With options, there is more risk to shorting. Technically, a stock can rise forever, while your downside risk is capped at the stock falling to zero. For this reason, many brokers explicitly display the warning that shorting or writing options is risky, and you should carefully consider the terms before choosing to do so.

This leads beginner options traders to conclude that selling (also known as writing) options is always risky when this isn't the case. It's true that writing options naked is an unintelligent move and is extremely risky. A naked option is a position where your downside risk isn't covered. However, if you cover your downside risk, writing options is one of the least risky things you can do in the markets.

For example, in our previous book, _Covered Calls for Beginners_ we highlighted the covered call strategy, which is another way to make extra cash when the market is doing nothing. This strategy requires you to write a call option while holding a long position on the underlying stock (this can also be an index or ETF). If the stock price goes up above your call option strike, you sell the stock at a profit, plus get the extra option premium. If the price goes down or stays the same, you get to keep your option premium.

Options offer many opportunities to build flexibility into your overall investing approach. It's why we favor using them in sideways markets. Writing options under the right conditions and within the right strategies is a good move because it allows you to take advantage of how options contracts are built.

If you're entirely new to the idea of selling options, here is the crucial point to remember at this stage; Buying options requires you to predict prices, but when you sell options you don't need to do so.

THE ADVANTAGES OF SELLING OPTIONS

The fact that you don't necessarily need to predict prices when writing options means you only need to predict if the underlying instrument (be it a stock or an index) will finish within a range. With the Rolls Royce example, we saw that predicting a price range is easier than an exact price. There are other advantages to writing options as well.

Time Decay is in Your Favor

Options contracts have a defined expiry date and have premiums attached to them. The longer there is until the option expires, the greater is the value of the premium. Therefore, options sellers are always in a position to capture the highest premium - no matter what happens to the underlying stock.

Upon writing an option, the seller keeps the premium, irrespective of what happens to the underlying. On the other hand, the buyer forfeits the premium, which forms a hurdle they need to overcome to make a profit. It's true that the underlying could always move to such an extent that the premium paid is negligible. However, that's moving into the world of directional trading. If you're going to be right predicting the direction of the market, you're just as likely to be wrong.

The option seller can be wrong as well, but there are ways to remove this directional dependency. First, the premium you pocket provides a cushion against losses. The key part of selling options is to cover the risk of the underlying moving against you. While it takes a little more understanding than your average stock trade, covering your downside risk means you can focus on predicting a price range, an approximate band within which the underlying will end up in, instead of needing to predict exact prices.

The second major advantage of this approach is you don't have to worry about whether you need to exit the trade or not. For example, if the underlying moves in an extremely volatile manner and reaches within a dollar of your profit target, you don't have to debate whether you should take a profit or not. In fact, by using the rule-based exit strategies we'll explain later, you don't need to even consider this scenario.

You Can Build Spread Trades

The strategies highlighted in this book are net credit spread options trades. These trades are part of a larger universe of trades called spread trades. Despite their ominous-sounding name, believe it or not, they're not as complicated as they sound.

We already discussed how by using options, you can bet on the markets' direction within a fixed period of time. Whether it will go up, down, or remain sideways. With net credit spreads, you remove the need for a directional bias in your predictions.

A huge benefit of no longer needing a direction bias is that your trades win more often. It isn't unheard of for spread traders to have eight, nine, or even 10 winning trades in a row.

This is because the profit amounts you earn are small but steady. Compare this to the boom and bust cycle that follows most directional traders, and you'll see how spread traders sleep much better at night.

Most directional traders have win percentages of 30-40%, or three to four winners out of 10. This is a stressful way to trade since win and loss distributions don't follow pre-ordained patterns. With a win percentage of 40%, it's incredibly likely that a trader will experience 10 losses in a row at a certain point. Losing money repeatedly and being able to still stick to one's strategy is tough to do. How many of us can genuinely claim to not care about 10 losers in a row?

Contrast this to the world of the spread trader. Your losses might be larger than your average wins, but they're far less frequent. This makes it easier to absorb from a mental standpoint. The probability of a long losing streak is close to zero, while an extended win streak is much higher. From a psychological point of view, spread traders find it easier to stick to their principles and make more money over the long term.

You Don't Have To Be Right

Credit spread trades don't require you to be right. You can guess a range of prices that the underlying will land in at the expiry date, and still make money. This alleviates a lot of pressure on your shoulders. If you've ever traded directionally, you'll know that one of the first rules of good risk management is to let go of the need to be right.

Successful directional traders truly let go of the need to be right and end up making a lot of money. However, the average trader who aspires to be successful finds this extremely tough to do. While it isn't an impossible target to achieve, it takes a lot of mental training and awareness to trade from true detachment from profits. The choice facing someone new to options is quite simple. You can choose to scale the directional trading mountain, or you can opt for an easier goal.

If there's an easier path to take, why not choose that instead of making things harder for yourself?

Lower Capital Requirements

Unlike other strategies which require a lot of capital to get going, it's relatively easy to get started trading credit spreads. You don't need to have much money in your account.

While this claim certainly isn't unique to credit spreads, in fact many stock and options strategies will tell you that you can get started with a small account. However, this is just a surface-level view and somewhat misleading. Dig a little deeper, and another picture emerges.

While you don't need too much money to open a brokerage account and start trading stocks directionally, you'll eventually run into the Pattern Day Trader rule (PDT). The PDT states that anyone who places more than four trades in a consecutive five-day period needs to maintain at least $25,000 in their trading account. This is an extremely high amount of money that the average retail investor doesn't have.

Most credit spread trades run for around 30 days. This means you can enter two or three trades over a week and have them run for a month. You won't be adding to these positions or subtracting from them in the interim. Most of them will close themselves out at expiry by expiring worthless, so there's no trade you need to place.

This keeps well away from the clutches of PDT. Plus, unlike covered calls, you don't need to buy underlying stock to cover your risk of writing options.

This means you truly can earn a steady income with a small amount of capital and with a few trades every month. Your trade setups will cover your downside risk automatically, so there's no need for you to post a maintenance margin, unlike with short stock trades.

You can get started trading credit spreads with as little as $1,000 in your account (theoretically, even starting with $500 is possible – although your choices will be more limited)

Win Probabilities

The success rate of credit spreads is high, as we mentioned earlier. It's not unheard of to have more than eight winners in a row. By our estimate, the hit rate of a solid net credit spread strategy is somewhere between 65-85%. Your precise win rate will depend on how you set up your trade and the kind of spreads you create. However, you can reasonably expect to land somewhere in this spot. As we highlighted earlier, this makes it a lot easier for you to trade within your rules, and you're less likely to get desperate and engage in revenge trading.

Synthetic Dividends

In our previous book on covered calls, we explained how you can generate what we call "synthetic dividends" by selling options. With covered calls, we wrote OTM options that were backed by long positions in the underlying stock. The premium that we earned by writing calls gave us income every month that was akin to receiving a dividend from our shares.

With credit spreads, selling options allows you to earn income, whether you own the underlying shares or not. Whether the underlying finishes in your target range or not, you still keep the premium you earned from selling the option, which acts as a handy buffer against losses. Over the long run, the income you earn from selling options provides an excellent additional boost to the capital gains from your long-term investments. This is what makes credit spreads such a powerful strategy.

Writing options also opens up the entire world of stocks to you. Many investors, especially those approaching retirement, are keen on generating income from their portfolio. Typically you would rely on dividends to do this. However, not every stock or fund pays a dividend. On top of this, many so-called dividend darling stocks like AT&T pay large dividends at the expense of low capital gains. Writing options allows you to buy a stock, whether it pays a dividend or not. If you're buying it for increased capital gains, you can still generate income on it. This allows you to capture the best of both worlds.

Defined Risk and Reward

The strategies you will learn in this book are what are called defined risk and reward strategies. You'll know your maximum risk and maximum reward before you enter the trade. Because of this, almost all brokers will allow you to sell credit spreads without needing any extra permissions on your account.

This feature contrasts with directional stock trading strategies where your reward and downside risk are not defined. While stop loss orders may claim to provide a veneer of risk protection, they're prone to get jumped by the market in reality, which results in traders realizing larger losses than planned. Stop loss jumps often happen when markets are extremely volatile, which is a Catch-22 situation because volatile markets are the condition that you placed your stop loss to deal with in the first place

Every directional trader faces a few moments of anxiety when the market hangs around their desired profit or stop loss levels without hitting them. In such times, traders need to decide whether they ought to take a lower profit and guaranteed money or whether they ought to let the trade run for longer. The only sure result is mental turmoil.

However, selling an option works differently. A credit spread trade has fixed risk limits thanks to the strike prices of your option. Unlike stop loss orders, the market cannot skip strike prices. They're a part of your options contract, and you're guaranteed that price no matter what. As long as the option hasn't expired and your position is ITM, your strike price must be honored.

This means your downside risk is always protected, and your maximum profit is also defined. By choosing the size of your spreads you can pick and choose your desired risk to reward ratios and design setups accordingly. You can trade with much greater freedom when you choose to set up credit spread trades. A huge unexpected move in either direction is not going to affect you.

You Don't Need To Be Present 24/7

The trading terminal is a constant companion of directional traders. Even during the off hours, they need to monitor news releases and volatility inducing events that might affect their positions' value. They need to track events like this because of the chance that their risk limits might be breached. If overnight volatility creates a gap in the markets on open the next day, their stop loss or take profit levels will not matter too much. If there isn't any liquidity in the markets, these levels will get jumped, and the consequences could be fatal to their account. Meaning that the average directional trader has to constantly make decisions.

This is not how credit spread traders operate. For starters, the length of an average credit spread trade is around a month. This means there's more time to operate, and you can take your time when analyzing your positions.

FREEMAN CREDIT SPREAD RULE #1

THE BEST CREDIT SPREAD SETUPS ARE ONES
WHICH DON'T REQUIRE YOU TO
SPEND ALL DAY MONITORING YOUR TRADES

The bottom line is that as an options writer, you do not need to be glued to your screen. In fact, with credit spread trades, allowing your trade to ride instead of grabbing whatever profits you can get is the best approach to make more money.

Now we've highlighted the benefits of credit spreads, let's dive in and see how they work.

CREDIT SPREADS ARE MUCH SIMPLER THAN YOU THINK

"I fear not the man who has practiced 10,000 kicks once. I fear the man who has practiced one kick 10,000 times."

— BRUCE LEE

T hanks to their name and the fact that their setups appear more complex than the average directional trade, credit spreads are often tagged as an "advanced" options trading strategy. This is a mistake as far as we're concerned. Credit spreads are much simpler than you think, and trading them is no more complex than setting up a basic directional trade.

New traders often get confused because of the large number of variants within the spread trade category. All spread trades can be classified into two major categories: net credit and net debit. In this book, we're looking at net credit spreads. These are trades which will put money into your account as soon as you enter the trade. Net debit trades on the other hand cost you money to enter, much like a directional trade does.

Generally speaking, net debit trades are far more directionally dependent than net credit trades. However, as we previously mentioned, most markets and instruments often move sideways or slightly upwards. They rarely ever move forcefully in any direction. This means a net credit spread is a better option.

Within the category of net credit spreads, there are over 25 ways to set up a trade. Traditional options education material list all of these strategies and expect beginners to understand them immediately. We believe this is a mistake. No one can learn two trade setups so quickly. It also propagates the false view that you need to create complexity in your strategies to succeed. In our view, there are just three net credit spreads that you should learn to make a solid amount of extra cash each month.

TRADE SETUPS

Before jumping into the individual trade setups that will make you money, we'd like to address another point of confusion. Spread trades are also classified as horizontal or vertical. Horizontal spreads (also called calendar spreads) are actually just a few trade setups, while vertical spreads have many setups within them.

A horizontal spread is constructed by buying or selling a near month option and also buying or selling a far month option of the same strike price. The idea is to assume the opposite direction in either leg. For example, if the near month option is sold, the far month is bought and vice versa. The type of option is also the same. Usually, calls are used, but it's possible to use puts as well.

A vertical spread on the other hand, is where you buy and sell options with different strike prices that expire on the same date. They are called vertical spreads because of the way option prices are displayed. Figure 1 illustrates this point.

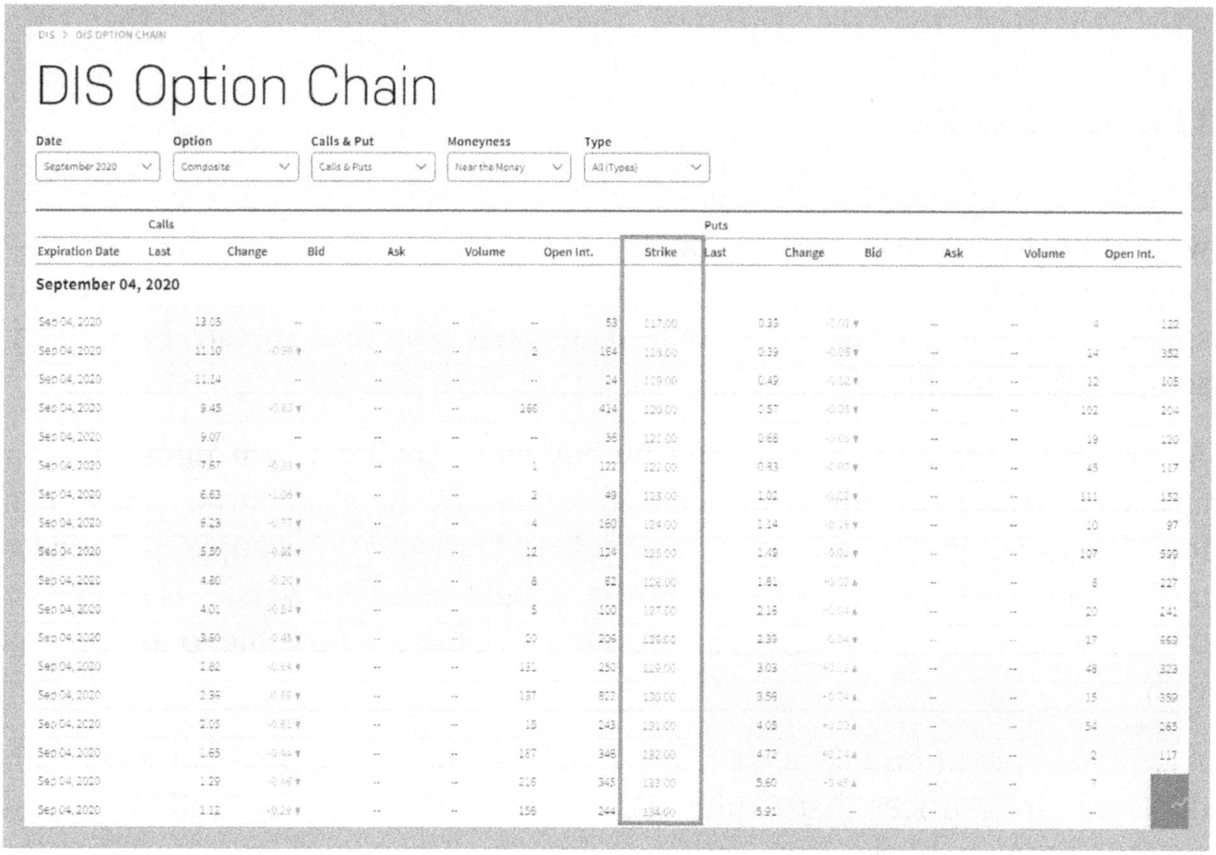

Figure 1: The Disney Options Chain for September 4, 2020 (Source: Nasdaq.com)

We'll be focusing on the three basic vertical net credit spreads. These three are the easiest to implement.

BULL PUT SPREADS

The first vertical net credit spread we'll look at is the bull put spread. The setup is vertical because all the options bought and sold expire in the same month. This trade setup has two legs:

- One short ITM put
- One long OTM put

As a refresher, ITM and OTM refer to "in the money" and "out of the money." A put is ITM when the underlying price is less than the strike price. The put can be exercised for a profit in this scenario. A call is ITM when the underlying price is greater than the strike price. Conversely, a put is OTM when the underlying price is greater than the strike price. A call is OTM when the underlying price is less than the strike price.

Writing the ITM option will put money in your pocket. Since it's ITM, you'll receive a large premium for it. The OTM option will cost you less and covers your downside risk. This setup allows you to profit from moderately bullish or range-bound conditions. If the stock price rises or it moves sideways in a range, the setup makes you money. Let's look at a hypothetical example to see how it works.

Say you're interested in SolarEdge Technologies (NASDAQ:SEDG), which is trading at $280. You don't know the exact price the stock will be in 30 days time. However you think it's likely to rise to $300 over the next month at the very least and that it's unlikely to fall below $265 in the same period. This is the "guessing a range" portion we spoke about in the introduction. Let's say the options are priced as below:

290 ITM put premium = $8

270 OTM put premium = $2

Writing the ITM put will net you $8 per share, while buying the OTM put will cost you $2 per share. Your net credit on entering the trade is $6 (8 - 2), which you will receive upfront. This is also your maximum profit on the trade.

Note: Remember that each option contract represents 100 shares of the underlying. So a credit of $6 per contract equates to $600 in your account.

Figure 2: How a Bull Put Spread is constructed in your broker. You are selling 1 OTM put option at 290, and buying 1 ITM put option at 270. For this example, we used the November 20th options, which had 26 days to expiry at the time the screen capture was taken (source: Tastyworks)

If your maximum profit is $6, what about your maximum loss on the trade? With credit spreads, your maximum loss is always equal to the difference between the strike prices of the long and short put, minus the premium you received for entering the spread. In this case, you wrote the short put at 290, and bought the long put at 270. Which means the distance between the strike prices is 20. Because you received $6 for entering the trade, and you get to keep this no matter what, therefore your maximum loss is $14 per option contract (20 – 6). Walking through various scenarios will help you understand how these numbers come about.

Scenario #1 - Let's say the underlying closes at $310 at expiry. In this scenario, your short put has finished OTM (since the underlying price is greater than the strike price.) It therefore expires worthless, and you get to keep the full premium. Meanwhile, your long OTM put remains OTM, and you will lose the $2 premium. Therefore, your profit is fixed at the $6 per share that you earned upon entry.

If the underlying closes at any price greater than $290, this is how much you'll earn. This is the maximum profit scenario.

Maximum profit = Premium earned from short put - Premium paid for long put = $(8 - 2) = \$6$ per share

Scenario #2 - If the underlying remains firmly in place, doesn't cross 290 and stays above 270 before expiry, here's what will happen. Your short put will remain ITM and your long put will remain OTM. Your short put will be assigned to you, which means you'll need to buy the stock from the option buyer for $290 per share. If the underlying is trading at $280, you'll carry an unrealized loss of $10 per share. You can either hold onto the stock and hope it rises back above $290 or you can sell it at the market price and eat the $10 loss. Your long put remains OTM, and you'll give up the premium paid.

Loss = Stock sale price - Short put strike price + (Premium received for short put - Premium paid for long put) = $(280 - 290 + 6) = -\$4$

You begin to lose money on this setup if the underlying closes below the short put upon expiry.

Scenario #3 - The third scenario occurs when the underlying finishes below the long put at expiry. If our stock closes at $260, here's what our options look like. The short put remains ITM and the long put also moves ITM. We'll need to buy the stock at $290 since this is the strike of the short put. However, we can sell the stock at $270 since the long option is now ITM. This means no matter how low the underlying moves, our loss is capped to $20 per share.

Loss = Strike price of long put - Strike price of short put + (Premium received for short put - Premium paid for long put) = $(270 - 290 + 6) = -\$14$

As you can see, the maximum profit is fixed and will be earned as long as the short put finishes OTM at expiry. This makes sense because the bull put spread is a strategy we employ when we are generally bullish on the stock's prospects.

Once again, each option contract equals 100 shares of stock, so a maximum loss of $14 per contract represents $1,400 in real terms.

Freeman Credit Spread Rule #2

Your best-case scenario is if both options finish OTM and the worst-case scenario is if both finish ITM.

BEAR CALL SPREAD

This is a bearish spread that looks to capture slightly bearish or range-bound movements in the underlying. Like the bull put spread, this setup has two legs to it:

- One long OTM call
- One short ITM call

Writing the ITM call will net you a premium that will be greater than the premium you have to pay for the OTM call. Like the bull put spread there are three scenarios that can result in either a profit or a loss with this setup. The first is if the underlying closes above the OTM call. In this situation, both calls will be ITM, and your maximum loss is realized. You'll have to sell the underlying at the lower strike price, but you can buy it at the higher strike, thereby capping your loss.

If the underlying finishes between the range within the two calls, your loss is equal to the price of the short call minus the underlying price. Your long call will expire worthless. The third scenario is if the underlying finishes below the short call and both options expire worthless. In this scenario, you'll keep the maximum profit, which is the net credit you receive on entry.

Let's look at an example to clarify how this works. We'll use the same numbers from our previous example. This time we are bearish on SolarEdge Technologies, which is currently trading at $280. So we buy a call at $290, and we write a call at $270. Our opinion is that the stock is going to fall below $270, but is unlikely to rise above $290. Let's assume the calls are selling for $8 (270 call) and $2 (290 call).

Figure 3: How a Bear Call Spread is constructed in your broker. You are selling 1 OTM call option at 270, and buying 1 ITM call option at 290. For this example, we used the November 20th options, which had 26 days to expiry at the time the screen capture was taken (source: Tastyworks)

Scenario #1 - The underlying closes at $300. In this case, both of our calls are ITM and we'll need to sell the underlying to the 270 option's buyer. However, we can buy the underlying at 290 thanks to our long call being ITM. Therefore:

Maximum loss = Strike price of short call - Strike price of long call + (Premium received from writing ITM call - Premium paid for OTM call) = (270 - 290 + 6) = -$14

Scenario #2 - The underlying closes between the two strikes. The long call remains OTM and the short call is ITM. Your loss is limited to the difference between the underlying price (let's say this is $280) and the ITM call's strike price, minus the credit received on entry:

Loss = Underlying price - Strike price of long call + (Premium received from writing ITM call - Premium paid for OTM call) = (280 - 290 + 6) = -$4

Scenario #3 - The underlying closes below both calls, moving them both OTM. In this case, you'll keep the full credit you received on entry. This is also your maximum profit on the trade:

Profit = (Premium received from writing ITM call - Premium paid for OTM call) = (8 - 2) = $6

Risk/Reward

Another feature of these two setups is that the maximum loss is far greater than the maximum profit. In both scenarios, our maximum loss is $14, while our maximum profit is $6. This gives us a risk/reward ratio of 42%.

If you've traded directionally, you'll realize that this is a highly skewed risk-to-reward ratio. In the directional world, such a strategy isn't worth sniffing at. However, remember that this strategy's win rate is much higher than what you can expect with a directional trade.

Let's say we have 10 trades with a risk/reward ratio of 30%, and we win eight out of 10 trades, with a max profit per trade of $100 and a max loss of $300. Assuming we either capture the maximum profit or suffer a maximum loss on our trades, our overall profit would be:

- Trade 1: Win +$100
- Trade 2: Win +$100
- Trade 3: Win +$100
- Trade 4: Loss -$300
- Trade 5: Win +$100
- Trade 6: Loss -$300
- Trade 6: Win +$100
- Trade 7: Win + $100
- Trade 8: Win +$100
- Trade 9: Win +$100
- Trade 10: Win +$100

So our net profit after 10 trades is ($800 - $600) = $200. An 80% win rate might sound fanciful for directional traders, but remember that with credit spreads you're not dependent on predicting the finishing price. You can increase your win rate to this level or more by constructing OTM spreads, as we illustrated just now. Your reward-to-risk ratio will fall, but you'll win a huge number of your trades.

FREEMAN CREDIT SPREAD RULE #3

THE CREDIT SPREAD STRATEGY IS ONE WHICH ALLOWS YOU TO MAKE SMALL, CONSISTENT PROFITS WITHOUT A LARGE AMOUNT OF RISK

This doesn't mean vertical credit spreads will result in wins 100% of the time. You'll need your options to expire worthless or you'll have to buy your short options back for prices lower than what you sold them for. Of course, if the trade moves against you, you'll only be able to minimize your loss and not avert it altogether.

SHORT IRON BUTTERFLY SPREAD

This setup is the third vertical spread we'll be looking at in this book. The name of this setup is confusing and, in fact, experienced options traders disagree on how to name this. You'll find them calling this strategy the long iron butterfly as well. To dispel any confusion, we wish to clarify that we're referring to the iron butterfly setup that results you establishing a net credit on entry.

The iron butterfly is a combination of a bull put spread and a bear call spread. The setup is designed to generate a profit from a sideways move in the markets, or mildly bullish or bearish moves. Like the Iron Condor, which we wrote about in our book _Iron Condor Options for Beginners_, the trade earns a profit in a specific range on both the long and short side. However, unlike the Iron Condor, the sweet spot is smaller. The flip side is that the maximum profit you can earn is a lot higher than what you can earn on the Condor.

There are four legs to an Iron Butterfly trade:

- 1 long OTM call
- 1 short ATM call
- 1 short ATM put
- 1 long OTM put

The key feature of the Iron Butterfly is that the short call and short put **have the same strike price**. This means the bear call spread portion of the trade and the bull put portion overlap with one another. If the underlying closes right at the strike price of the two short legs, you'll realize your maximum profit. You might think that this means you need to predict price, but this is not true.

What happens is that the short legs, since they're written at the money (ATM), generate a large premium that gives you a range within which the stock can finish and still yield you a profit. It's just that to realize the maximum profit, you need to predict the price accurately. In this setup, the maximum profit isn't realized as often as on the two-legged vertical spreads we discussed earlier. However, since the trade combines two vertical spreads into one, your average profit is a lot higher than on a two-legged spread trade.

Let's look at an example to see how this works. Currently, Visa (NYSE:V) is trading at $200.99. We'll set up our Iron Butterfly as follows:

- Buy one $190 put for $1.98
- Sell one $200 put for $5.40
- Sell one $200 call for $6.10
- Buy one $210 call for $2.34

The credit we receive on entry = Premium received from writing the 200 call + premium received from writing the 200 put - cost of the long 190 call - cost of the long 190 put = (5.40 + 6.10 - 1.98 - 2.34) = $7.18 per share. Each options contract carries 100 shares of the underlying with it. This means our credit totals to $718.

The maximum loss this trade will realize is the difference in the strike prices between the long and short options legs, minus the premium received on entry. When constructing the trade, the distance between the long and short legs of the trade needs to be equidistant in both spreads. The distance between the long and short call should be the same as the distance between the long and shot put. In this case, this distance equals $10.

The maximum loss is = (Distance between strike prices - credit received on entry) * 100 shares per contract = (10 - 7.18) * 100 = $282

Since we receive a credit on entry, the trade has a buffer to it. This means our upper break even limit is the strike price of the short put plus the credit received:

Upper break even limit = Strike price of short put + net credit received = $200 + $7.18 = $207.18

Similarly, the lower break even limit = Strike price of short call - net credit received = $200 - $7.18 = $192.82.

The reward profile of the Iron Butterfly is illustrated in Figure 4 below.

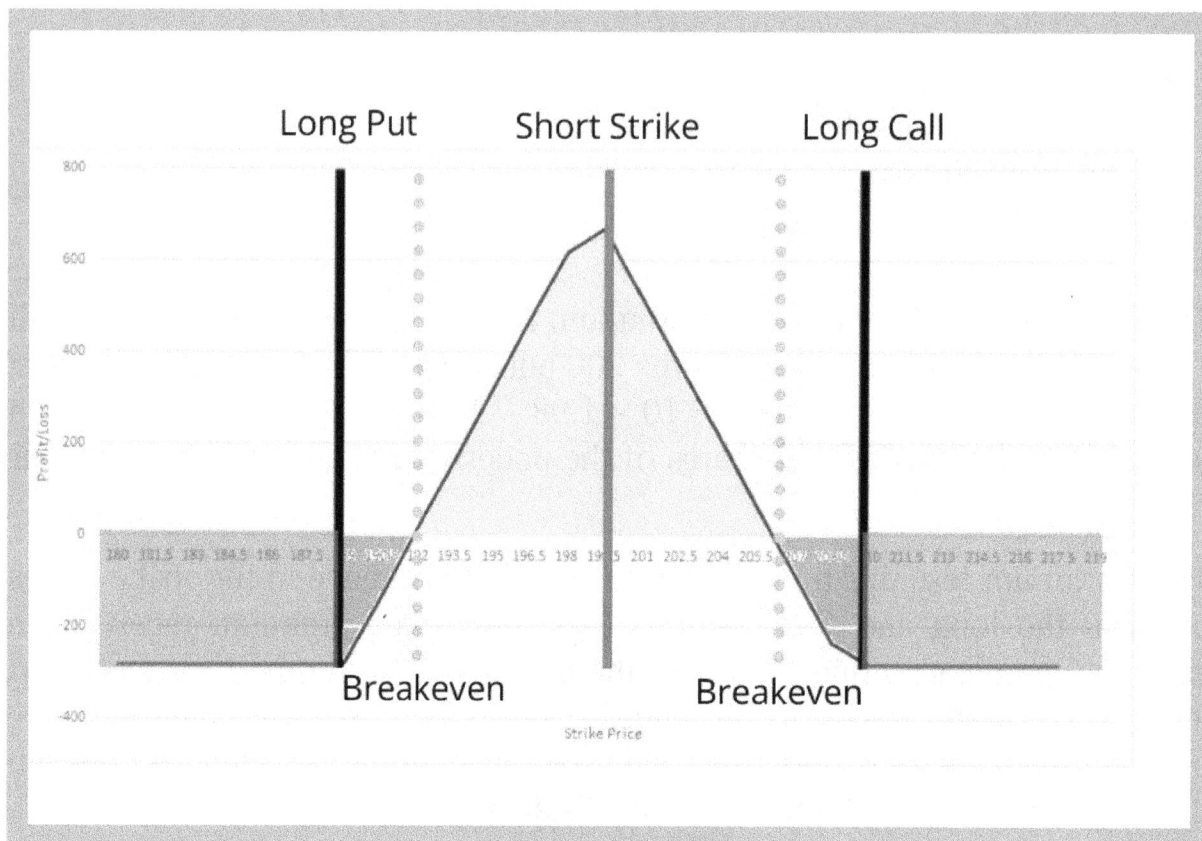

Figure 4: The Above Short Butterfly Spread Visualized

As long as the underlying finishes between $192.82 and $207.18 at expiry, this trade will be in profit. This is the profit range that we alluded to earlier. The maximum profit, which is the net credit realized on entry, is realized if the stock finishes at exactly $200 at expiry.

A more realistic scenario is that the price will finish somewhere close to it and we'll net a profit that is slightly lower than our maximum profit. The maximum loss is realized if the stock finishes outside the strike prices of the long call or put. These long positions limit our losses in the trade.

While you can set up the trade with ITM short calls, you can technically build a directional bias into the trade. For example, if you think the stock you're looking at will fall and then move in a range, you can set up the Iron Butterfly at a lower price than the current stock price and choose strike prices in such a way that your predicted range will be equal to your break even limits.

As with credit spreads, you can create wide butterflies, which increase your probability of a win, but your reward-to-risk ratio will decrease.

POINTS TO NOTE BEFORE TRADING CREDIT SPREADS

There are a few issues you need to consider before trading these three setups. The first is to see whether you can trade these within an IRA. The answer is yes, but it depends on your broker. Generally speaking, brokers allow you to trade defined risk strategies within your IRA. The above 3 setups are considered defined risk, since the long options legs limit your loss, your broker should allow you to trade them. If you are unsure, or your account doesn't appear to allow you to sell credit spreads, then call your broker on the phone and ask them to enable credit spreads in your account.

The next issue is one of trade management. What if you enter the trade and find that your assumptions are incorrect or that the trade is moving against you? We'll deal with this in great detail in the chapter on trade management. Managing your options trades is simple when you do so from a rule-based perspective. We'll give you all the rules you need to consider before changing the structure of your trade.

The next and perhaps biggest issue to consider is that of early assignment risk.

Early Assignment Risk

You'll notice that in all of these setups, we're writing ITM options. Generally speaking, options are not assigned (when the buyer exercises their ITM option and converts their option into shares of stock) until expiry. However, it's not as if this can never happen. By writing an ITM option, we're constructing a trade that requires the stock to move a certain distance before we can realize our maximum profit. This involves a certain degree of risk.

For instance, let's assume that when constructing our bull put spread, the underlying does move to a level that pushes both options OTM at expiry. However, if the ITM option was assigned to us well before expiry, at a point in time when the underlying was still in between the two strikes, we'll take a loss on this trade (Scenario #2 in our previous examples.)

Every once in a while, this will happen and will cause you to take a loss despite being right about the market's direction.

To mitigate this risk, you can construct your spreads at different levels. In the case of the bull put spread, you're assuming that the stock will rise. Since you're writing an ITM put, you need the underlying to move above the ITM put and push it OTM. What if the stock doesn't rise or if you're assigned the option before expiry? To mitigate this risk, you can construct the spread differently. Instead of writing an ITM put, you can write an ATM or slightly OTM put.

From our example, the underlying was trading at $280. Instead of writing a put at $290 (which is ITM), you can write a put at $280 or $275. The long put can be bought at $270 as in the example. In this scenario, if the stock finishes in place or if it moves slightly higher, you'll still capture the maximum profit. Early assignment won't be possible since your short put is already OTM. An ITM put can be assigned, but stock price fluctuations will likely move it OTM at some point.

Similarly, when constructing a bear call spread with the underlying at $280, you can buy an OTM call at $300 but write a call slightly OTM at $285. In this situation, the stock needs to move by at least $5 to push you into a loss. Early assignation isn't a risk since both of your calls are OTM. If you wrote an ITM call, you'd begin in a position where your trade might result in a loss if the option is assigned early to you.

The flip side is that you'll exchange a lower maximum profit for the safety that these spreads bring, because OTM options will sell for less than ITM ones. However, if you're worried about early assignment, you can opt to construct spreads like this. There is no hard and fast rule that you have to write ITM options. Doing this gives you greater profits, but you open yourself up to the slim possibility of early assignment.

While early assignment is a risk, it doesn't occur, for the most part. Why is this? It has to do with the extrinsic versus intrinsic value of options. Intrinsic value is the difference between the underlying price and the option's strike price. An option only has intrinsic value if it is ITM.

Let's use Las Vegas Sands (NYSE:LVS) as an example. The stock currently trades around $55. If we buy a $50 call for $6.50, then we have $5 of intrinsic value (because the stock is worth $5 more than the option we bought), and $1.50 of extrinsic value (the price of the option minus the intrinsic value.)

If we buy a $60 call for $1, then we have $0 of intrinsic value because the option is OTM. However, since we could resell the option for $1, it still has $1 of extrinsic value.

Therefore an OTM option has only extrinsic value since it has zero intrinsic value. What this means for early assignment is that by exercising their options contract, the buyer gives up all the extrinsic value that the option has. Which means the majority of the time, if the option buyer exercises their contract early, they only capture a fraction of the profit they could realize.

For example, let's say your short ITM call with a strike of $290 was exercised 40 days before expiry. Once it is exercised, the option has zero extrinsic value. What if within 40 days, the price of the underlying rises to $300? By exercising the option early, the buyer can capture the rise in stock price from 290 to 300. However, the option premium will likely generate them a higher profit because it will gain intrinsic value while maintaining its extrinsic value as well, to a large extent. Extrinsic value will decline sharply within 30 days of expiry. Exercising beyond this range doesn't make sense.

In fact, even within the 30 day to expiry period, it isn't as if extrinsic value evaporates. Volatility and other market conditions result in an option having some degree of extrinsic value. Giving up this profit doesn't make sense.

The key to remember is that early assignment only happens in rare circumstances. You can also mitigate early assignment risk by trading cash settled index options (like SPX or RUT).

CHOOSING A BROKER

As easy as it is to just trade credit spreads using your regular broker, it's worth figuring out if there is a better option.

There are a few elements you need to consider before choosing a broker. Let's look at them one by one.

COMMISSIONS CHARGED

Commissions are a considerable headwind to overcome when it comes to trading. With options, there are two tiers of commissions you need to be aware of. The first is the cost of buying and selling options. This cost is similar to the commissions you'll pay when buying or selling stocks. Brokers have different structures for them, so you'll need to check which one makes the most sense for you.

Most brokers will list per contract commissions, but some will have a model where you'll pay a fixed charge up to a certain level and will then pay additional fees when you trade above this threshold. Thanks to the rise in discount brokers, these most brokers don't charge commissions on trading options contracts. They might charge fixed contract fees, this means you won't pay commissions, but you might pay 70 cents per contract. That sounds like it could get expensive, but most brokers have a maximum price per trade. For example, the contract fees on Tastyworks are capped at $10 regardless of the trade size.

Not every broker will charge you contract fees, so this makes your choice a little more confusing. Take the time to consider your trading volume and look at the fee schedule that the broker advertises. At the very least, you can expect to pay zero trading commission fees since there are so many app-based options that charge zero commissions.

The second type of fee you'll pay when trading options is assignment fees. Once again, some brokers charge zero assignment fees, but this isn't always the case. Assignment fees are what options sellers pay. Options buyers pay exercise fees. It's the same fee, except the name changes depending on which side of the trade you've assumed.

Add these fees together to take your final commissions paid into account. One broker might charge zero commissions but higher assignment fees. Remember that these fees eat away at your profits, so you need to be aware of them before trading.

When you're just starting with 1-2 contracts per trade, your total trade fees shouldn't add up to more than a few dollars.

SOFTWARE

Broker trading terminals vary greatly. The best brokers to pick are the ones who cater exclusively to active traders. These companies have the most sophisticated tools. Having said that, the platforms that these brokers provide can be quite complex, so you don't want to choose one that requires you to go through a steep learning curve.

Avoid choosing brokers who cater to long-term investors. Long-term investment is a different game entirely, and most investors don't need sophisticated charting tools or options visualization tools. In fact, many long-term investors don't even need a real-time chart.

This is not the case for options traders. Not only do you need real-time charts, you also need risk profile visualization tools like the one we highlighted in Figure 4. These tools help you enter proposed strike prices, and you'll clearly be able to see your break even points and maximum profit and loss scenarios.

You don't need standalone desktop terminals to execute these strategies. You'll be spending perhaps a few hours every month maintaining these setups, so it's not as if you need a supercomputer to make them work. A web-based software is more than enough for your needs.

Another factor to add is to make sure your broker has a good options calculator. You'll need this to walk through various scenarios.

There are great third party calculators such as the one available at optionsplaybook.com. You can use a broker that has zero or low commissions and pair it with this calculator for maximum benefit.

If your broker's charting interface is clunky, then you can use a resource such as tradingview.com. This free software allows you to draw support and resistance zones, and use technical indicators you'll need when analyzing possible setups. We'll be talking more about these later on in the book.

One more important consideration for you to consider is your broker's experience in dealing with options trading. The more experienced brokers will allow you to enter both legs of your credit spread trades at once. This makes execution and capturing optimal prices much easier than entering each leg one at a time. It also insulates you from sudden bursts of market volatility. If you were entering your legs one at a time, you might find yourself having opened one leg with the other out of position, and the numbers on your trade will have changed.

CUSTOMER SERVICE QUALITY

This should go without saying, but you need to choose a broker with a high level of customer service. Unfortunately, these days, most customer service queries are handled by chatbots. This is frustrating because you'll need to speak to a human every once in a while. Evaluating how quickly you can access a human being is an excellent metric to measure different brokers.

You can check this by typing a few questions into the chatbot software and then checking to see how soon the bot connects you through a human. If it keeps you going round in circles, then it's a good indication that the company doesn't take customer support seriously enough. Many companies will ask you to leave your number and request a callback. This isn't good enough. If your situation is an emergency, you can hardly be expected to sit around waiting for a phone call from your broker.

Another way of evaluating their service is to send them an email and look at how long they take to get back to you. In most cases, the initial response will be quick. Send a follow-up question and wait for a response. By doing this, you're checking to see what kind of customer service process the company has. Most brokers figure that once initial questions are answered via email, the person asking them ends up opening an account. This leads them to not follow up on secondary emails.

The lack of response indicates poor after-sales service, and you should stay away from such brokers. The longer a broker has been in business, the better their customer service will be.

Choose a broker that has been around for a long time and read their reviews on impartial websites like Trustpilot. Always choose a broker that is registered with the Financial Regulatory Authority or FINRA. If you're just starting out, avoid offshore brokers since all kinds of illegal and unethical behavior is possible with them.

CUSTOMER EDUCATION

Most traders don't look at the educational resources their brokers provide, and strictly speaking, you don't need these resources to succeed. However, they're a good indicator of where the broker's priorities lie. A broker that spends resources on providing free learning tools, webinars, and other educational content clearly cares about the quality of their customers' orders.

Brokers who cater to active traders typically don't invest in such resources. This doesn't mean those brokers are bad. It's just that they cater to experienced, active traders and their platforms will probably have a certain degree of sophistication that might make it difficult for you to trade immediately. Choose a broker that offers a variety of resources and you'll be just fine.

MARGIN REQUIREMENTS

To trade vertical spread options strategies, you'll need to open a margin account. This might sound intimidating if you come from a background of "margin is always bad". But don't worry, you won't be borrowing money to trade. In this case, a margin account simply refers to having enough money in your account to cover any potential trade losses.

Margin allows you to write options, and you'll have to have enough in your account to cover any potential loss. Most brokers will automatically sell ITM options at expiry if you don't have the margin to exercise them. Assignment is also done automatically. You'll receive a notice of assignment, and your account's positions will change to reflect the situation. If you're trading index options, everything will be settled in cash since you can't own an index.

Brokers typically have four or five levels of accounts that you can open. Each level determines what sort of strategies they'll allow you to trade. Buying options and writing covered calls can typically be done with a level one account without any hassle.

Because credit spreads involve selling options on assets you do not own, you will usually need a level three account. Gaining approval to open these accounts depends on your trading experience and the margin in your account. However, this is usually as simple as answering a few questions on the phone or ticking additional boxes when you open your account. Credit spreads are a risk defined strategy, so brokers do not have many hurdles which prevent you from using them.

This is why it's essential that you choose a broker who is well versed in options trading strategies and has a good amount of resources dedicated to options traders.

FEE SCHEDULE

In older times, many brokers used to get away with hiding fees within their fee schedules. This doesn't happen anymore, thanks to increased transparency. However, a few hidden fees still sneak in. For example, some brokers may charge an account maintenance fee every month if your total margin is less than $10,000. This isn't advertised as a minimum margin penalty, of course, so most people miss this fact.

There are other little fees that add up. Wire transfer fees, account statement fees, dividend check payment and legal document fees can add up over time. A good broker will post a clear and easy to understand fee schedule on their website and will also mention it in their terms of service agreement that you'll sign when you open an account.

Pay special attention to the quality of the broker's software. If it's glitchy and regularly hangs, you'll need to phone in your trades. Most brokers charge a fee for this, and it can be as high as $25 per trade. Inactivity charges are another way that brokers will make money off you. This is especially the case with brokers who target active traders. If you're transferring your balance from one broker to another, watch out for transfer fees.

These are the primary features of a broker that you must consider before choosing one. These days it's quite easy to read reviews of brokers and to figure out what their customers are saying about them. Take special note of the negative reviews. Not all of them will be legitimate, but an unusual number of reviews that mention the same problem is a good sign of something wrong with that broker.

Many brokers offer signup bonuses. These are usually free cash deposits to your account or a few commission-free trades. It's important that you ignore these promotions when choosing a broker. They don't tell you anything about the quality of service you'll receive. Always keep the quality of service and the experience of the broker in mind when choosing one.

BROKERS WE RECOMMEND FOR CREDIT SPREAD TRADING

Note: We are not affiliated with either of the companies listed below. Brokers and fees change all the time, so be sure to double check before you open an account

- Tastyworks by Tastytrade
- $1 per contract to open (capped at $10 per trade)
- Cheaper fees for trading index options
- Zero commissions to close
- Can open/close both legs of the trade simultaneously
- Easy to set up take profit targets
- Free ACH deposits & withdrawals
- Excellent education platform
- Available to European users
- Thinkorswim by TD Ameritrade
- Commission free trading for US stocks & options
- $0.65 per contract
- No assignment fees
- Easy to use software
- US users only

"CAN I USE ROBINHOOD OR WEBULL TO TRADE CREDIT SPREADS?"

We get this question from email subscribers quite a lot, as many of them are using Robinhood or WeBull to buy stocks.

The answer is… yes, but we don't recommend it.

Newer app-based solutions such as Robinhood and WeBull are a decent starting point for investing, but they're poor choices to execute credit spreads with.

For starters, you need a computer screen to execute these setups. You cannot reliably execute them using a 6" phone screen and expect to be successful. Trying to construct and manage a multiple leg strategy on a cell phone screen isn't ideal.

Combined with the fact that neither of these platforms has phone support if anything goes wrong (as you'll see in our later chapter on Tesla options), neither Robinhood nor WeBull is a good long term solution.

FREEMAN CREDIT SPREAD RULE #4

TAKE TIME IN CHOOSING YOUR OPTIONS BROKER. THIS WILL PREVENT UNNECESSARY STRESS OR FINANCIAL LOSS.

Now we've covered opening your account, let's dive deeper into understanding how to maximize your profits. First we'll cover the often-misunderstood world of option Greeks.

OPTION GREEKS IN 10 MINUTES

Entire books are written on option Greeks. To be frank, we could have written one ourselves. The Greeks are a great way of distilling the most important risk factors of option pricing into easily understood numbers.

By "easily understood" we speak relatively, of course. From your perspective - that is, of a market participant who has some experience with options, but isn't looking to complicate matters too much, delving deeply into all the Greeks' characteristics is pointless.

We've highlighted three strategies for you to follow in this book, and as a result we'll be highlighting just the Greeks that make the most sense for you from a trade entry and management perspective.

Keep in mind that it's possible to go even more in-depth with the Greeks than what we've covered here. Our objective is to emphasize all the relevant features that you should pay attention to for credit spreads. The first options Greek that we will use is Delta.

DELTA

Delta (Δ) measures the rate of change of an option's price relative to a price movement in the underlying.

For example, if a stock is trading at $100 and one of its calls is trading for $1, a movement in the underlying from $100 to $101 can hardly be expected to move the price of the call option from $1 to $2. That would mean a one percent move in the underlying price would result in a 100% move in the price of the call. If this were true, options would be a gold mine for everyone.

While the call might not move to that extent, it does move in some proportion to the price of the underlying. Delta gives us an exact value for how much this move will be. Delta values always range from -1 to 1 (although they are sometimes expressed as a percentage on broker platforms). Technically speaking, they range from -1 to 0 for put options and from 0 to 1 for calls. Put deltas are negative because they gain in value as the price of a stock falls.

For example, let's say we have a stock trading at $100 with a 105 strike call that is trading for $1 with a delta of 0.5.

The first thing to note is that the delta value is specific to the option, not to the underlying. Meaning options with different strike prices will have different deltas. The call with a strike price of $105 might have a Delta of 0.5, while the call at $110 might have a delta of 0.3. This means for every dollar's worth of movement in the underlying, the 105 and 110 call prices will increase by 50 cents or 30 cents, respectively.

This means if the stock moves from $100 to $101, the 105 call would be worth $1.50 and the 110 call would increase in value by 30 cents.

Similarly, if a put's delta is -0.4, the put's value would increase by 40 cents for every dollar's drop in the underlying's price. Many people make the mistake of reducing the value of the put for a price drop in the underlying due to the negative sign. However, since the value of the put increases the more the underlying drops, the put's value increases with the increase in delta.

As the price of the underlying fluctuates, so does the delta for each option. Several factors are a part of the delta calculation. The most important of them all is implied volatility or IV. This number will be listed in the option chain and is usually represented as a percentage.

Volm	Delta	Bid	Ask	Strike		Bid	Ask	Delta	Volm
Nov 27, 2020 W			Calls	33d	Puts	Last			IVx: 27.1% (±19.55)
4	0.60	13.47	13.57	340		8.32	8.39	-0.40	54
1	0.58	12.80	12.90	341		8.64	8.72	-0.42	0
15	0.57	12.13	12.24	342		8.98	9.06	-0.43	19
36	0.56	11.81	11.91	342.5		9.15	9.23	-0.44	0
7	0.55	11.49	11.57	343		9.33	9.41	-0.45	11
129	0.54	10.85	10.93	344		9.69	9.77	-0.46	52
358	0.52	10.23	10.31 ITM	345		10.07	10.15	-0.48	1.15K
280	0.51	9.62	9.70	346	ITM	10.46	10.54	-0.49	7
155	0.49	9.03	9.11	347		10.87	10.95	-0.51	3
41	0.48	8.74	8.82	347.5		11.08	11.16	-0.52	1
116	0.48	8.46	8.53	348		11.29	11.37	-0.52	1
33	0.46	7.90	7.97	349		11.73	11.81	-0.54	1
373	0.44	7.36	7.43	350		12.18	12.28	-0.56	17
POP	EXT	P50	Delta --	Theta --	Max Prof	Max Loss	BP Eff		

Figure 5: The SPY options chain with 33 days to expiry. You can see the deltas for each strike price with the call deltas on the left and the put deltas on the right. You can also see the implied volatility (27.1%) for the underlying in the top right hand corner. (Source: Tastyworks)

The IV represents the expected volatility in the stock. The greater the expected volatility is, the more expensive options traditionally are. This is because deltas increase with IV and, therefore, the price fluctuations of the options contracts increase with them. Since they're so closely tied to IV, the value of an option's delta also approximates the probability that it will finish ITM at expiry.

This means an option with a delta of 0.4 has a 40% chance of finishing ITM. We must point out that this is an approximate measurement, and there's no definitive way of predicting whether an option will finish OTM or ITM at expiry. However, you can use delta as a good proxy for figuring out how likely your option will remain OTM when you write it.

As an option moves closer to expiry, the delta of an ITM call option will move closer to 1 (-1 in the case of a put.) If the option is ATM, delta will hover around 0.5 for calls or -0.5 for puts. Once the option is OTM, delta will begin sliding towards zero. Note that the rate at which delta changes might accelerate as the contract slides towards expiry. This is especially true if the stock is volatile. In that case, you might see an option delta drop precipitously from 0.5 to 0 if it moves from being ITM to OTM.

Deltas can be extended to entire strategies as well. For example, the bear call spread is a negative delta trade since the delta of the short option will be greater than the delta of the long position. This makes intuitive sense since the setup is a bearish one that gains value if the stock slides. A bull put spread will have a positive delta because it's a bullish setup. The Iron Butterfly is a delta neutral strategy since the deltas of each leg of the trade will cancel one another.

GAMMA

Gamma (Γ) confuses a lot of traders and is often pointed to as evidence that trading options is complicated. Like every other facet of options trading, you can complicate gamma as much as you like. First, let's define what gamma is. Gamma measures the rate of change in an option's delta. Instead of measuring anything to do with the underlying price, it measures the rate at which delta changes.

For example, let's say we have an underlying stock trading at $100 and an OTM call at $105 selling for $1, with a delta of 0.5 and a gamma of 0.02. This means if the underlying moves from $100 to $101, the 105 call premium will increase from $1 to $1.50, and the delta will increase from 0.5 to 0.52. This makes intuitive sense because as the underlying gets closer to the strike price, the probability of finishing ITM increases. This means the closer the underlying price moves to the strike price, the higher delta goes. Not only does it go higher, but it also accelerates faster as well since gamma increases as well.

However, gamma's movements aren't as intuitive as delta's are. It's a second derivative of price and relating gamma back to price can get complicated. To make it easier on ourselves, we learn to think in terms of the probability of an option finishing ITM.

Gamma accelerates as an option moves from OTM to ATM. Once the option moves from ATM to ITM, it begins to decrease. Examining the behavior of delta will help us understand why this is. As an option moves from OTM to ITM, delta moves towards 0.5. It moves faster as the price inches closer to the strike price. As the option moves from being ATM to ITM, its delta moves closer to 1 (or -1 in the case of a put.) The closer it moves to 1, the shorter the distance it has to move. Therefore, its rate of change decreases as well. Hence, gamma decreases, the more an option is ITM. At some point, the delta will be 1 and it can't go higher than this. As delta stops moving, so does gamma, and it settles to 0 value.

Time also plays an important role in determining how gamma behaves. An ATM option's gamma increases as expiry draws closer. This means the probability of an ATM option finishing ITM increases dramatically as expiry draws closer. The effect of gamma decreases as we move further ITM or OTM.

In this way, we can look at gamma as a measure of certainty. The further ITM or OTM an option is as we move closer to expiry, the more confident we are that the option will finish ITM or OTM respectively. When certainty is high, gamma is low and vice versa.

Gamma tends to accelerate with less than 7 days to go before expiry. Suppose you enter the last week before expiry with options that are slightly OTM. In that case, gamma can increase rapidly, thereby pushing delta higher, which in turn indicates that the probability of your option finishing ITM will be high.

A small move in the underlying can produce exaggerated movements in the price of the option as a result. This is why it's best to avoid trading credit spreads for weekly options since gamma can leave your positions precariously placed.

Notice how gamma for Disney options changes in Figure 6 depending on the amount of time left to expiry.

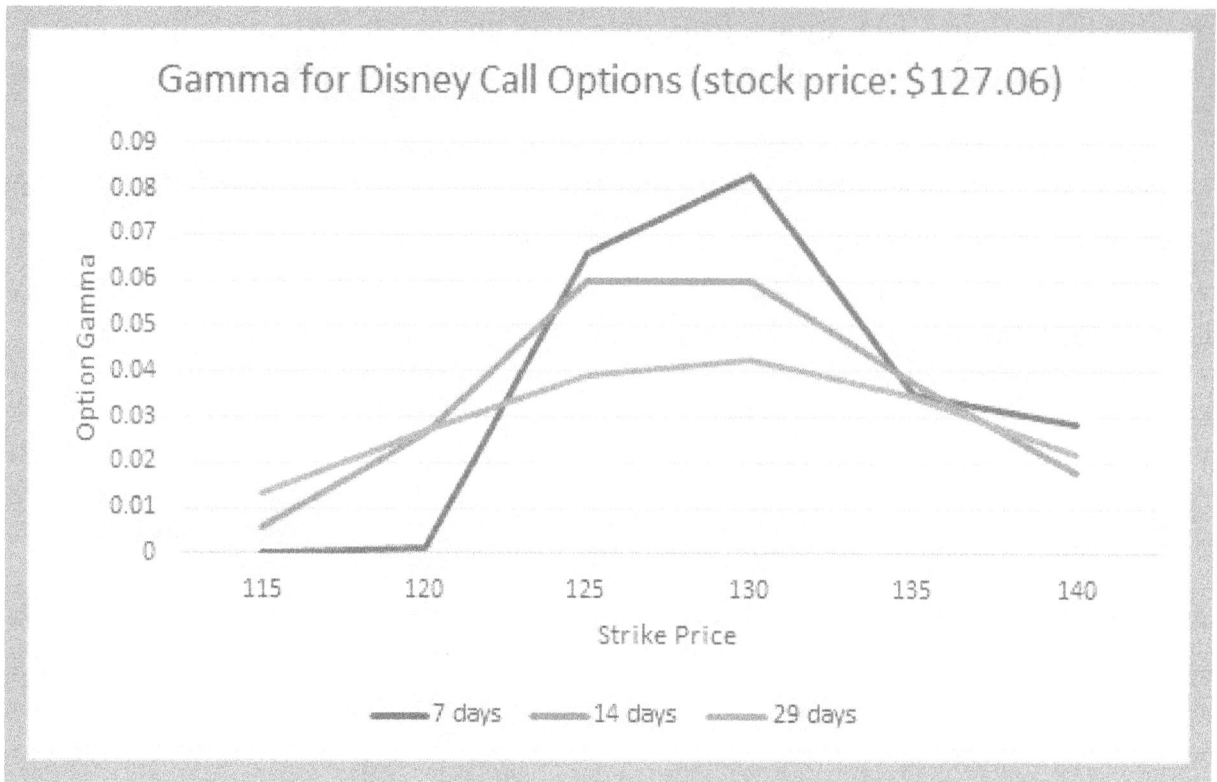

Figure 6: Gamma for different strike prices of Disney Calls at 3 different time periods

The calls that are slightly OTM at the 130 strike price and that have just 7 days to expire have the highest gamma. Note how the 130 strike has the highest gamma irrespective of how many days are left till expiry. Also notice how each curve's slope changes dramatically depending on how many days are left till expiry. The options that have just a week left will take their owners on a rollercoaster ride thanks to the degree with which gamma rises and falls.

It can take a while to fully comprehend the impact gamma has on your positions, so take some time to read this section once again. At the very least, recognize that the final week until expiry is the most uncertain time for you. If your position is near the money or not deep enough OTM, it's best to close your position and take whatever profits you have instead of trying to bet that your options will remain where they are and make you money. Closing your trade out also removes the possibility of a leg being assigned to you. We'll discuss exactly how we like to do this in the chapter on trade management.

THETA

While gamma and delta deal with the effect of the underlying on the option's price, theta measures how time affects the option's price. Theta (Θ) is used as a proxy to measure time decay, which is why you'll sometimes see time decay referred to as "theta decay." Options are intricately connected to time. Every option contract has a certain date beyond which it is worthless, which affects how it is priced.

Think of it like this. An option with 200 days left till expiry and is OTM, has more time to move ITM than an option that has the same strike price but has just one day left until expiry.

This means the latter option will be worth much less than the former. Figure 7 illustrates how this affects the way options are priced.

Financial Instrument	Bid	Ask	Account	Action	Quantity	Time in Force	Type	Lmt Price	Status
SPY Dec18'20 343 C...			DU2497404	BUY		1 DAY	LMT	14.17	Transmit
SPY Oct16'20 343 CA...			DU2497404	BUY		1 DAY	LMT	7.04	Transmit
SPY Sep18'20 343 C...			DU2497404	BUY		1 DAY	LMT	4.07	Transmit
SPY Aug31'20 343 C...			DU2497404	BUY		1 DAY	LMT	1.24	Transmit
SPY Aug26'20 343 C...			DU2497404	BUY		1 DAY	LMT	0.41	Transmit

Figure 7: The option premiums for an OTM 343 call option for the SPY ETF with different times remaining until expiry. (source: Interactive Brokers)

Let's look at an example. If the underlying price is $100 and its 105 call is priced at $1 with a theta of -0.2, the premium will decrease by 0.2 everyday. Theta represents a decrease in the option's price, and this is why its value is negative. Note that theta can fluctuate. As an option gets closer to expiry, theta accelerates exponentially.

Theta decay is what all options sellers look for. It's a proxy for measuring the extrinsic value an option has. The further OTM an option is, the more extrinsic value it has. As this option moves closer to expiry, the less value it has, and as theta decays, the extrinsic value drops exponentially. In fact, the last 30 days till expiry is when theta decreases the most, and we'll discuss how to take advantage of this in the next chapter.

For now, just note that as a net option seller, theta is your friend. If you write an option outside the 30 days to expiry window, you'll be capturing as much of the premium as possible. As the days go by, the premium's value accelerates to zero, and you can keep more of the premium. Since the price of the contract decreases exponentially, you can keep more of the profit even if you cover your position. It's merely selling high and buying low.

Theta accelerates, and this causes an option's price to drop significantly in the month leading up to expiry. This is why we like writing credit spreads that expire in 30-45 days since we can capture maximum theta without exposing ourselves to additional risk.

EXPIRATION DATES

Now that you understand how the Greeks work a little better, expiration dates are easier to address. A common concern amongst options traders is picking the correct expiration dates for their positions. Most experienced credit spread sellers choose to open positions that are 30-45 days away from expiry. This time frame is often provided as a default period as well.

Given the effects of theta and gamma we covered in the last chapter, you can now see why this period is optimal. An option that is greater than 45 days away from expiry won't witness too many price movements, and as a result you'll simply keep twiddling your thumbs waiting for something to happen. Options that are this far out often aren't very liquid either, so you might enter at prices that aren't optimal.

Once the option moves into the 45-day window, more traders start taking a look at it, which automatically boosts its liquidity and the rate at which gamma, theta, and delta move. This, in turn, brings even more traders on board and makes it easier to evaluate the case for entering a position.

Given that delta is a good measure of how likely an option is to finish in the money, it's a good idea to look at values that are as accurate as possible for it. An option that is more than 45 days away from expiry isn't going to have precise delta values, much less gamma.

Theta will remain pretty much constant since any price moves in the underlying will be negated by the fact that there's still a lot of time left until expiry. If the option moves ITM or OTM, there's still a ton of time left for the option to go the other way. Therefore, as an option seller, your money is pretty much stuck in the position doing nothing.

For this reason, we recommend that all of the positions you open be between 30 to 45 days away from expiry. This will allow you to both evaluate the option properly and you'll be able to capture the highest possible premium before theta starts rapidly decaying and decreasing the option's premium.

	Volm	Delta	Bid	Ask	Strike	Bid	Ask	Delta	Volm
Oct 30, 2020 W					5d				IVx: 36.6% (±)
Nov 6, 2020 W					12d				IVx: 43.2% (±)
Nov 13, 2020 W					19d				IVx: 43.7% (±)
Nov 20, 2020					26d				IVx: 43.8% (±)
Nov 27, 2020 W					33d				IVx: 43.1% (±)
Dec 4, 2020 W					40d				IVx: 43.3% (±)
Dec 18, 2020					54d				IVx: 45.0% (±)
Jan 15, 2021					82d				IVx: 45.6% (±)
Feb 19, 2021					117d				IVx: 46.9% (±98.05)
Mar 19, 2021					145d				IVx: 45.9% (±108.42)
Jun 18, 2021					236d				IVx: 47.0% (±138.85)
Jul 16, 2021					264d				IVx: 45.5% (±142.82)
Sep 17, 2021					327d				IVx: 47.2% (±161.02)
Jan 21, 2022					453d				IVx: 49.0% (±185.25)

Figure 8: The Netflix options chain showing days to expiry. For credit spreads, we would look at the November 27th (33 days to expiry) and December 4th options (40 days to expiry). This allows us to capture as much of the premium as possible without holding our position during periods when options prices are doing nothing. (Source: Tastyworks)

There are some events you need to watch out for, however. It's not as if you can simply open a position 30 to 45 days away from expiry and expect it to work out. The technical state of the underlying stock matters, and we'll cover this in detail shortly. The other factors to watch out for are special events.

SPECIAL EVENTS

Special events are huge factors when it comes to analyzing volatility. When it comes to selling options, volatility is both your friend and enemy. If it turns against you, it can result in a position that was profitable for the majority of the contract, suddenly turning into an unprofitable position right before expiry.

We'll discuss the specifics of volatility in more detail in the next chapter. For now, let's look at some events that create volatility in the markets and how you need to tackle them.

Earnings Announcements

We've now established that the lifecycle of your options position is going to be between 30 to 45 days long. It is essential during this time that there be no earnings releases scheduled. The markets eagerly await earnings announcements and there's a lot of natural volatility in stock prices before them. In fact, stock prices reflect many expectations before the release is announced, which affects how the options are priced.

For example, if a stock is expected to announce record breaking earnings, its options will be priced higher than usual because the market will expect the stock price to move quickly in a given direction. If the company announces record earnings and it's a company that is followed extensively by the retail trading crowd, the price is bound to shoot higher. If it disappoints, you can expect institutional traders to pummel the stock, and the price will drop. The only thing in the markets worse than having expectations is having bad expectations affirmed. Whatever happens, the stock is going to move by a large degree, up or down. It certainly isn't going to move sideways or go anywhere slowly.

None of this fits the criteria that we need for our three setups. The vertical credit spreads require mild to sideways conditions, and the Iron Butterfly aims to capture sideways moves. Even a moribund stock that largely moves sideways isn't a good candidate during earnings season. Companies use these announcements to make other announcements regarding the future direction of the company. The reports are also accompanied by a flurry of insider trading.

In the stock market, insiders have to declare their positions and cannot trade based on insider information. If they get caught doing this, the penalties are large. A large insider move before disappointing earnings is a red flag. Therefore, most insiders schedule their trades right after earnings are announced. Of course, if earnings are great, the stock could go rocketing up on insider buying. However, we're not concerned with up or down. Volatility and consistency are what we're after. The more consistent volatility is, the easier a stock's option chain is to trade.

You can find earnings announcements calendars in your broker's software. Most often, they will be denoted with an "E" symbol in the options chain or on the stock's price graph.

Alternatively, you can visit the investor relations section on the company's website and look at the information presented there. Most brokers will have alerts set up to notify you of special events occurring with a stock you are monitoring.

FREEMAN CREDIT SPREAD RULE #6

DON'T WRITE CREDIT SPREADS ON A STOCK
WHICH HAS AN EARNINGS ANNOUNCEMENT
IN THE MIDDLE OF YOUR TRADE

Dividends

Dividends often get lumped together with earnings, but they deserve their own section. This is because, in the days leading up to the dividend payment, the amount of the dividend is accounted for in the stock price. If the stock will go ex-dividend (the date at which the stock will trade without the added value of the previous dividend amount) during the lifecycle of your trade, its calls will be priced lower to account for the dividend and you won't be able to capture as much premium.

Special Announcements

You'll need to pay attention to a company's business to figure out whether there is the possibility of a special announcement injecting volatility into proceedings. For example, pharmaceutical companies live and die by the results of their research. As a rule of thumb, you want to stay away from these companies because so much of their business hinges on approvals and lengthy drug trials working out.

The average drug spends around 8-10 years to move from inception to hitting the market (Frazier, 2015). Imagine working on a drug for close to a decade only for it to be rejected. This is a huge reason for these stocks being volatile. The pharmaceutical giants have many drugs under development, and this smooths their results, but smaller firms rocket up and down.

It isn't just pharmaceutical companies that are subject to such announcements. Announcements regarding restructuring, the results of a lawsuit or the results of a shareholder vote, create massive volatility in a stock. You don't want to be in the market using the three strategies in this book when volatility hits.

Since the predominant focus on the net credit spread strategies is to earn premiums, you need volatility to remain stable or decline. If a company is in any condition where it needs to make a special announcement that could affect its fortunes, you need to stay away from it.

Special note must be made of company CEOs who use Twitter to make major announcements instead of using the usual press release route. The rise of Silicon Valley has caused many CEOs to think they have a moral duty to disrupt everything in sight, for the sake of disruption. It's best to stay away from such scattergun CEOs who shoot their mouths off on social media. For the purpose of credit spreads, stick to boring companies with boring businesses. They're more likely to move sideways anyway.

Economic Releases

Economic releases happen all the time, so it's hard to avoid them. The ones you want to avoid are the major ones, such as interest rate announcements and jobs report releases. Both of these events occur once a month, so it may seem impossible to avoid them on a 45-day cycle. There is some good news, though.

First, these announcements are more significant for index options than they are individual stocks. They still affect company stocks but not to the extent that company-related announcements do. Therefore, you can always write options on individual stocks during these periods. If you're trading index options, try to time your positions within a 30-day window so that you can avoid these announcements.

Special note must be made of events related to the Federal Reserve Bank, such as their annual summit at Jackson Hole. These events are usually the source of major political and economic announcements, so you need to steer clear of them. While it hasn't occurred over the past decade, you also need to watch out for emergency meetings of the Federal Reserve.

This typically happens when a major bank has undertaken too much risk and is exposed to total collapse. In such situations, the markets become incredibly chaotic since the trouble hits banks directly. These events don't always make the headlines, but if you're even remotely connected to the market, you'll be aware of them. It's impossible to predict these events in advance. The best you can do is exit your positions for whatever you can get and capture as much profit as you can instead of exposing yourself to more turmoil.

Political Events

Politics interferes with everything, and the markets are no different. Election outcomes can affect the volatility of the markets. Thankfully, it's just the presidential election you need to watch out for. Of course, since 2016, sources of political volatility have been varied. While political leaders have been extremely careful with their statements regarding the stock market in the past, this isn't true anymore, with outrage fueling election campaigns. The markets don't react to every tweet or soundbite released, but you should be aware of important political dates or announcements.

As the world moves forward, the prospect of a trade war between America and China seems increasingly permanent. This means any companies that have links to China or whose business hinges on American government approval are risky. For example, many chip makers and semiconductor stocks such as Huawei have been badly affected due to their products being sourced from China but sold in the US. With these companies effectively having to pick sides in the argument, their stocks will be more volatile than ever.

These are just a handful of events that could affect your position. There are many more than can be covered here, and you'll need to evaluate how much a particular event can affect a stock's prospects. Remember that you want to err on the side of low volatility at all times. The best situation is if a stock is transitioning from a high volatility situation to a low volatility one. This will mean that premiums will be overpriced when you buy and underpriced when you sell. You'll earn bigger profits thanks to the greater price difference.

However, don't rely on such stocks all the time. It's easier to choose truly snooze-worthy ones that don't create any surprises for their stockholders, and you'll generate steady income for many years from them.

Now that we've covered events that affect volatility, let's further examine how we can use volatility levels to our advantage.

IMPLIED VOLATILITY DEMYSTIFIED

I mplied volatility, or IV, is another concept that is central to options trading success. There are many explanations on the internet about what IV is and how options traders should use. The problem is that, like much of options trading, IV can be made as complicated or as simple as you wish. Most explanations of IV tend to focus on the mathematical explanations, which are often counterproductive.

Before we focus on how IV affects credit spreads, it's essential to understand what volatility is and how this affects stock and options prices. We've already covered the implications of volatility before, but let's revisit it. Volatility is just the degree to which an instrument's price will move in a given direction. A stock whose price jumps around all over the place is more volatile than one that moves steadily in one direction.

Volatile markets are dangerous places for traders, and as options sellers, we're not interested in operating in risky environments. In fact, all three strategies we've highlighted seek to take advantage of sideways moves and market conditions that are the enemy of directional traders. For this reason, volatility is not our friend.

The ideal situation is if volatility is high at our entry point and then decreases. This reduces the values of the Greeks and also reduces the movement in options prices. This in turn, increases the odds that our options will finish close to their original buy or sell prices, and we get to keep as much of the premium we earned as possible.

The entire market has a measure of volatility that many traders follow. This is called the volatility index or VIX. So if you're trading index options, you'll need to keep tabs on the VIX. From an individual stock's perspective, the VIX doesn't affect the price much. If you're trading individual stock options, then the stock's implied volatility is far more important.

THE ROLE OF IV IN OPTION PRICING

The phrase "implied" provides us a good idea of what IV is all about. It's represented as a percentage and is typically quoted on the option chain itself. It signifies what traders think of the current volatility levels in the stock and its future prospects. If a stock is expected to be volatile, the IV will be high. If it's expected to move sideways, its IV will be low. You can compare a stock's current IV to its historical IV levels to get an idea of where it currently stands.

On a more technical note, IV is the measure of the odds of the stock trading within one standard deviation away from its current price. That's a convoluted definition, so let's look at how it works via an example.

Disney is currently trading at $128, with an IV of 26.1%. This means there is a 68.1% chance (we'll explain why 68.1%, and why this is a crucial number later) of Disney trading within 26.1% of $128 over the next year.

The range of possible prices extends from 26.1% below the current price to 26.1% above it. These numbers are $94.50 and $161.

Note that Disney has a 68.1% chance of trading in this range. All IV numbers are interpreted this way. They give us the range that the stock has a 68.1% chance of trading in within a year. Do not confuse this with 100%. There is always a chance that Disney could trade outside this range as well. Another factor to pay attention to is that IV doesn't discriminate in terms of direction. It gives the stock an equal chance that it could trade above the current price or below it.

In practical terms this means the lower IV is, the smaller the range that a stock is predicted to trade between. When it comes to option prices, generally speaking, the higher the IV is, the more expensive that stock's options are. This stands to reason. Using our numbers from the Disney example, a call with a strike price of 160 is OTM at the moment, but it's within the IV range. This means it has a good chance of moving ITM over the next year. Therefore, as the expiry date lengthens, the premium attached to this call's strike price will increase. If we're in September right now, the October expiry will be priced pretty low. However, next September's 160 call will be priced high because it's more likely that Disney can hit that level within the next year.

The distance of the strike price combined with the time left to expiry plays an important role in the option's pricing, as you can see. Generally, deep OTM options will be priced cheaply, irrespective of their expiry date. This is because IV indicates that they're unlikely to move ITM.

As credit spread traders, we'll be buying and selling options, so the IV of one leg of the trade will cancel the other out. However, since our target is to earn as much of the premium as possible, it's in our interest to sell options that are OTM, but that can give us high premiums. This is why many traders are willing to risk selling ITM options on trade entry and risk assignment because the payoff is larger. Selling borderline OTM options is another way you can increase the premium you earn.

You must be careful though. If you do this repeatedly with high IV stocks, you're taking a high risk of the option finishing ITM. This is why it's best to target stocks that have high levels of IV from which they're certain to descend. You'll earn the resulting premium caused by high IV and will then be well placed to keep most of it as IV decreases and the stock begins to reduce in fluctuations.

It's important to note that common advice mentions that it's best to sell options in high IV environments. This is only half the story. While selling it is a good move, if IV keeps increasing, you're not doing yourself any favors. What you want is for IV to *decrease* as the trade progresses.

Ideally, you want IV to be below 50% when entering your trade. Stocks with an IV above 50% are usually too volatile to ensure consistent returns.

To give you a practical look at the kinds of IV levels to expect when analyzing stocks, here is the IV for the following nine instruments at the time of writing

- AT&T – 17.3%
- SPY (S&P 500 ETF) – 18.3%
- Costco – 25.3%

- Microsoft – 25.5%
- IWM (Russell 2000 ETF) – 27%
- Tesla – 56.3%
- American Airlines – 62.9%
- Moderna – 77.2%
- Nio – 143.1%

As you can see, more volatile stocks like Tesla, Moderna and Nio have much higher IVs than broad market ETFs or "boring" stocks like AT&T and Costco.

As you can see in Nio's case, a stock can have an IV of above 100% if it is incredibly volatile. You should never write credit spreads on a stock with an IV above 100%.

Factors That Affect IV

Calculating IV is less important than understanding the various ways in which IV can change given market conditions. The most obvious factor that affects its value is supply and demand. The higher the demand for an instrument, the higher its IV will be. Again, note that IV does not indicate direction, so if there's a lot of supply in the market, IV will be high as well.

Many people think low demand environments automatically indicate low IV values, but this isn't correct. If supply is high and there are more potential sellers than buyers, the stock can slide dramatically, increasing the option's IV. Instead, a balanced supply and demand environment is what causes a drop in IV. This is because there are an equal number of buyers and sellers in the market, so the stock is likely to move sideways.

Another market condition that creates low IV is low supply and low demand. This usually happens when a stock has been moving sideways for a long time, and traders (most of them directional) aren't interested in it anymore.

Time until expiry is another major factor in determining IV. The closer an option is to expiry, the lower its IV is. This makes intuitive sense because the closer the option is to expiry, the less time it has for the price to move significantly. The more time an option has until expiry, the higher the premium is. However, this doesn't mean you need to sell options that are expiring 100 years from now just to capitalize on higher IV. The objective is to earn as much premium as possible and capture it as quickly as we can. This is why the 30-45 day window works so well.

Market conditions also play a role. If the entire market is highly volatile, even low volatility stocks will have high IV values. In such conditions, you need to check whether the market 's volatility is likely to affect the underlying stock's price movement a lot. If the stock in question is highly connected to the market's overall health, you need to track the VIX closely.

For example, at the time of writing, the S&P 500 index is highly influenced by the stock prices of the FAANG stocks (Facebook, Apple, Amazon, Netflix, and Google). If the VIX is high, it's basically measuring the collective IV of these stocks. Even if one of them has been historically low in terms of volatility, the weight it carries regarding the overall index will push its IV higher. If you're trying to capture a premium in a decreasing volatility environment in this stock, you need to pay attention to the VIX as well as overall market trends.

That's all there is to learn about IV. If you're feeling overwhelmed at this stage, don't be. The most important thing to remember is that to profit from the strategies highlighted in this book successfully; you only need to learn where to find IV values in your broker software. You don't need to know all the intricacies of how they're calculated.

FREEMAN CREDIT SPREAD RULE #7

IF YOU'RE UNSURE ABOUT IV LEVELS, STICK TO STOCKS WITH AN IV OF LESS THAN 50%.

CLARIFYING MISCONCEPTIONS ABOUT TECHNICAL ANALYSIS

Technical analysis is a potent tool, but it'll be a hindrance rather than a help if you cannot use it properly.

Here is the good news, for credit spreads, you don't need complicated indicators. The truth is that it's possible to identify stocks that make good credit spread candidates using a simple moving average. It sounds impossible, but it's true.

Another piece of good news is that technical indicators tend to remain evergreen (at least most of them do) because they're closely related to the order flow of the underlying. So it's not as if you need to learn new chart patterns every other week. As a rule of thumb, the more removed a technical indicator is from price and order flow, the less reliable it will be in the long run.

But what about these super-intelligent, multi-billion dollar quantitative trading firms? Don't they use extremely complex technical algorithms to make trading decisions? Or what about these High Frequency Trading firms which come into the news every so often. Aren't they hiring the best and brightest minds to program technical algorithms all day?

There is much misconception surrounding High Frequency Trading (HFT) and algorithmic trading amongst ordinary investors and traders, so let's spend some time dissecting how these firms make money.

WHY YOU SHOULDN'T FEAR ALGORITHMS

First, we'd like to make a distinction between your average quantitative trading strategy and what a HFT firm does. Many quantitative trading strategies trade in ultra short timeframes, but this is not what we refer to when we speak of HFT. HFT firms, by our definition, are front runners. The edge that these firms have isn't technical wizardry but just deep pockets.

Here's how these firms work. They co-locate their servers as close to the exchange's matching engine as possible and rely on their orders hitting the market before the average trader's order does. Let's say you place an order to buy 100 shares of Wal-Mart at the market price. Your broker will pass this to a stock exchange clearing firm. These firms are responsible for executing the large volume of orders they receive, and that's it. They aren't brokers, and their sole objective is to find the best prices possible.

Let's say the first 10 shares of your order are filled on the NYSE at $150 each. There are still 90 shares left in the order, but there aren't any more shares of Wal-Mart available on the NYSE. This isn't a problem because the clearinghouse can search the NASDAQ. If the NASDAQ cannot fill the orders, there's BATS. If not BATS, there's the NYSE ARCA and so on. There's no shortage of stock exchanges, and it's not hard to fill orders of any size.

The HFT firm has prior knowledge of the order in which clearinghouses hop between exchanges. We'll explain why shortly. They co-locate their servers at all the exchanges in advance and lie in wait. When they see your order of 100 WMT hitting the NYSE, they know that this order will need to hop elsewhere. Before the clearinghouse hops to the NASDAQ, the HFT firm buys all the WMT available and lies in wait. As your order (via the clearinghouse) hits the NASDAQ, the HFT increases the price by a fraction of a cent and sells it to you (Lewis, 2015).

This doesn't sound like much of a profit, but if you multiply this by millions of orders a day, you'll realize that an HFT firm can clear billions every year without ever taking a loss on their trades. There's no analysis magic here, just a lot of money poured into high speed infrastructure. You might wonder how the HFT firm knows of your order size when it hits the stock exchange? After all, the clearinghouse isn't advertising the order size, is it?

Well the truth is that HFT firms buy order flow data from exchanges. It's how stock exchange companies make as much money as they do. It's also a big reason why you don't pay commissions on stock purchases or option trades anymore. Your broker is selling your order flow information to an HFT that is fleecing you fractions of a cent every time you trade. As sordid as this picture is, there's nothing you can do about it unless you open a billion-dollar fund of your own and specify which exchange you want your order to be routed to. So just think of it as the cost of doing business.

The point of all this is to show you that there's no technical analysis going on with HFT firms. They're front running your order, and that's it. Their actions have no impact on technical indicators.

What about the algorithmic traders, though?

Algorithms

Algorithmic trading firms operate in two markets, broadly speaking. These are the stock and bond markets. But what many investors miss is that the ratio of activity between these markets is roughly 95:1 in favor of the bond market. (*Bond Algos Tap into ETF Liquidity and Efficiency Gains*, 2019). Why is this? Simply that the bond market dwarfs the stock market in size by many multiples. It's populated exclusively by institutional traders, and there is next to zero retail presence. Think of it as a top-tier sports league, and the division below representing the stock market. Most algorithmic trading firms are institutions themselves.

This automatically means they gravitate towards the bond markets. There's another powerful attraction that the bond markets have. There are no insider trading laws that govern it. Many of the protections you take for granted in the stock market don't exist in the bond market. This makes it easier to trade if you have the resources. The retail side of the market greatly affects the price movement of many stocks.

Algorithmic traders by definition, are looking to trade on a rational basis. They collect large sets of data and develop models with them using sophisticated technology. The presence of a 20 year old with a brand new

Robinhood account who doesn't know the difference between a long and a short corrupts this data. After all, this person isn't acting on rational principles. They're trading purely out of emotion. They're buying TSLA because they saw the price was going up and heard they could potentially double their money within a few days. No one can create a model out of that.

As a result, algorithmic trading in the stock market is restricted to market making or applying other techniques such as order cloaking. Market making is what clearinghouses do. They're straightforward execution desks and aren't concerned with technical patterns. All they're doing is getting their clients the best prices they can find.

The most important thing to note is that you, as someone selling credit spreads for extra income, have nothing to fear from these firms.

Order cloaking, or to use the illegal version of it, order spoofing, is a method by which a trader masks their true intentions. They might place an order to buy 100 shares, but their intention might be to sell 10,000. Many order spoofers and cloakers try to catch HFT firms napping and they typically do. There is no actual technical analysis going on here. Order spoofers reverse-engineer HFT algorithms, which as you've learned don't use technical analysis.

So where does this leave us? The algorithms that use sophisticated technical analysis are far fewer in number than you might initially think. You are free to develop more sophisticated methods than ever, but the truth is that as long as you stick to indicators and intelligently use them, there's no need for you to overcomplicate technical analysis. To trade credit spreads, you don't need to worry about algorithms snatching away advantages from you. Neither do you need to develop special indicators.

Despite what "professional traders" trying to sell you a $3,000 technical analysis course might tell you, the markets aren't some treasure chest that can be unlocked with a magical key. Many people try it, and a few even succeed in designing algorithms that make them daily profits. However, as we've repeatedly mentioned, it's far easier to pick trading ranges and use options to profit from them instead of trying to catch market lows and pick tops. This is what makes trading credit spreads so powerful.

HOW TO USE TECHNICAL ANALYSIS FOR CREDIT SPREADS

While many traders try to time the market using technical analysis, our opinion is that it's far better to use technical analysis to identify the periods when the market is doing "nothing" from a directional trader's perspective. These periods are greater in number, and in addition to using technical analysis, you'll be able to visually spot such periods as well.

It's not very hard to look at a chart and determine whether the instrument is moving sideways or in a particular direction. Even if this isn't clear, the technical analysis indicators you can use to determine such periods are pretty simple to plot and decipher. When it comes to making extra income with credit spreads, simplicity always wins. You can use complicated indicators, but just because an indicator is complex doesn't mean it's accurate.

A common argument for using new indicators is that no one else in the market uses them. This is falling back into the "secret key" type of thinking that dooms many traders. The markets are too random for one indicator to consistently give you spectacular returns. Instead, you need to regularly use those that help you detect patterns in the market's behavior. Counterintuitively, the indicators that do this the best are some of the oldest and simplest ones.

The next chapter will introduce you to the indicators we recommend using to trade credit spreads. Our data proves that these indicators are perfect for these setups. In our research, we haven't found any instances of a complicated indicator being more accurate in any way than the ones we will highlight in the next chapter.

THE THREE TECHNICAL INDICATORS YOU NEED TO KNOW

Before we dive into individual indicators, it's important to take a step back and remember why we're even using technical analysis. In our case we're merely using it to figure out whether the market is trending or ranging. Often, the market rests in between these two states.

The most common method of figuring out a trend's direction is to draw trendlines. They're intuitive and are an easy way of figuring out which points the market might touch as it moves in a given direction. Take Figure 9 for example.

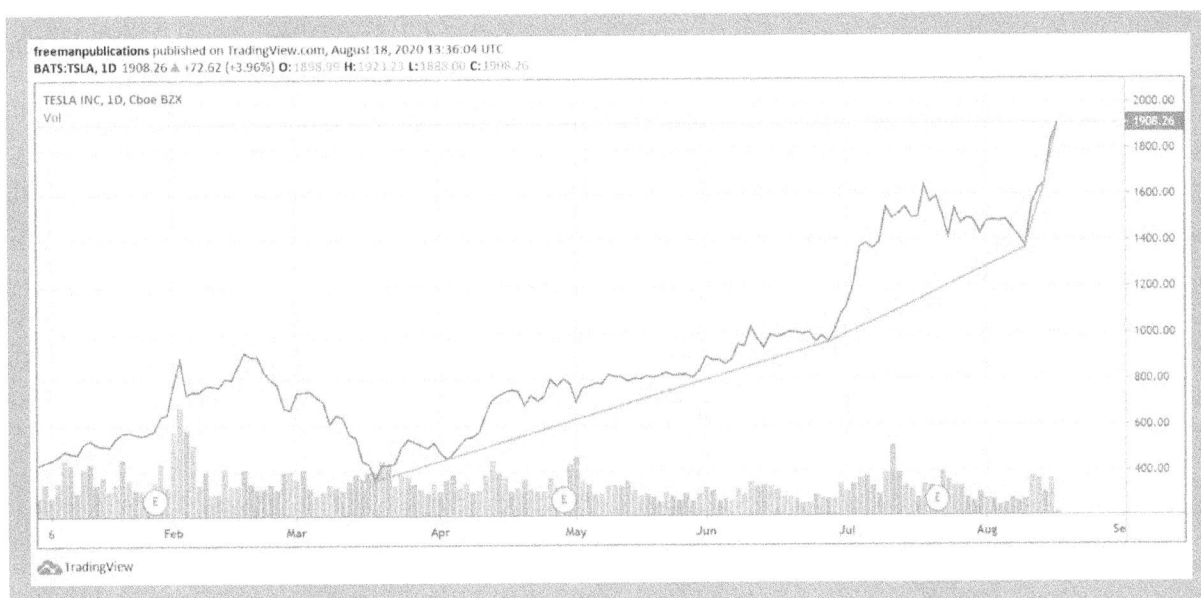

Figure 9: Trendlines in TSLA for YTD 2020 (pre-stock split). (Source: TradingView)

It doesn't take a genius to figure out that Tesla was rocketing from March to August 2020. The problem with trendlines is that they're incredibly subjective. When trends are as clear as they are in Figure 9, it's easy to connect the dips and figure out which ones are relevant.

However, the market is rarely ever this clean. If the price action is messy enough, you can reasonably draw more than one trendline through a price action sequence and have multiple trendlines indicating different trend strengths. This does nothing to help us figure out which way the stock is trending. Even in Figure 9, which is a clean set of price action, you can see that we've ignored many of the medium term dips the market made.

Choosing which dips to consider and which ones to ignore takes experience, and this is something newer traders don't have. As a result, drawing trendlines isn't the best idea. There's also the fact that the best trendlines are drawn in hindsight, which does nothing to help us predict which way prices are going to go.

Closely related to trendlines are price channels. If one trendline is hard to draw, drawing two of them to form a channel is even harder. Many trading education books depict clean channels, but these are usually the result of selective picking. In reality, you'll be hard-pressed to find stocks that lend themselves to perfect price channels.

Instead, we can start with the easiest and most reliable indicator, namely support and resistance levels.

SUPPORT AND RESISTANCE

Technically speaking, support and resistance levels are not an indicator. However, they're indispensable. The fact is that many trading authorities misrepresent them. Support and resistance levels are a great way to figure out the order flow prevalent in a stock (or any financial instrument). This helps us choose the right strike prices for our options.

The market is composed of many traders, and every one of them has a certain opinion on what prices ought to be. These traders have different strategies and are operating in different time frames. As a result, a consensus is hard to achieve. This is why when areas on a stock chart show that many traders agree on price, it's significant. These areas are where support and resistance lines should be drawn.

An example of this is illustrated in Figure 10 where the 9 EMA acts as a dynamic support during an uptrend. The stock price continues to bounce off this level through the year-long period of price increases.

Figure 10: An Example of Dynamic Support on SPY (Source: TradingView)

Price Swings

Prices swing from one side to the next all the time. These swing points are vital since they tell us that the market was pushed in a particular direction by traders and that these traders were overwhelmed by traders from the other side of the market and that prices were pushed right back. Traders remember these levels, so when they see these levels where prices were pushed the other way in the future, you can reasonably assume that there will be another bounce.

When levels are broken, the zones where prices previously bounced will be retested from the other side. For example, a swing low that acts as a support will be broken, and prices will retest the level from below as resistance. More often than not, these levels work as strong resistance. Similarly, once a strong resistance level has been broken it acts as support. See figure 11 for a visual example of this.

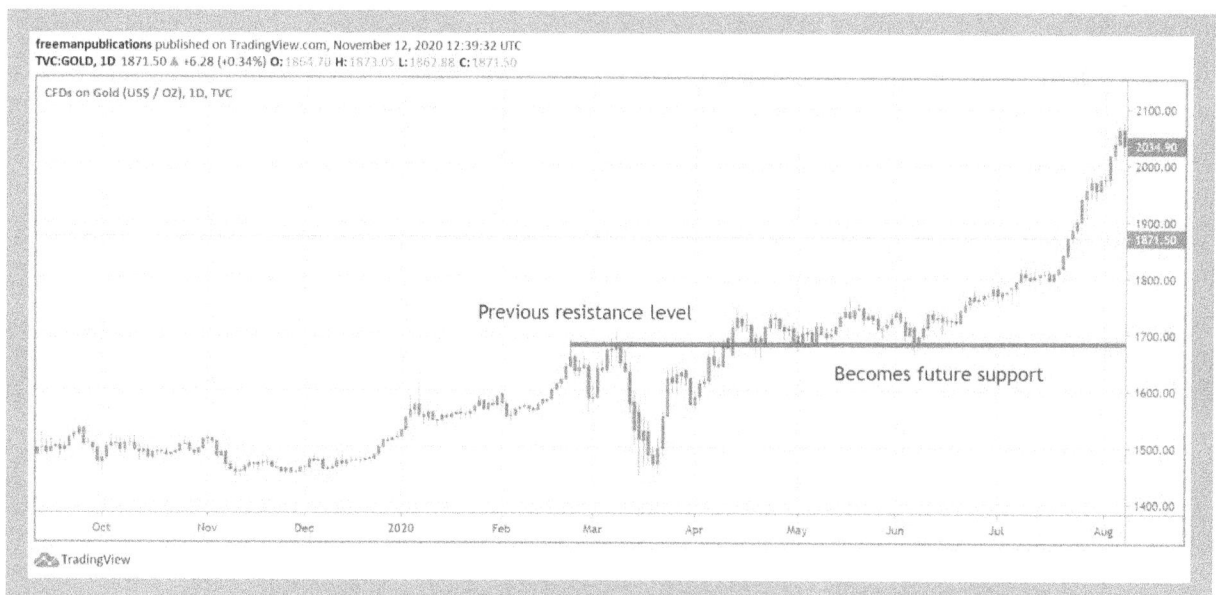

Figure 11: Gold price breaks through the previous resistance level of $1,690, which then becomes the new support level (Source: TradingView)

The reason these levels are robust is because of the number of traders who look at them. The more substantial support and resistance levels are the ones that have a large number of traders waiting near them. The easiest way to spot the strength of a level is to look at the force with which price approached it and its reaction. If the price hit the level after approaching it steeply, this indicates a lot of force behind the move.

If a move with that much force can be countered and pushed back, it indicates that the traders waiting at that level are much stronger. Therefore, it's likely that there will be a secondary reaction when price retests it. When evaluating swing points, look at the angle with which price approached the level and the angle at which it left it. This is the easiest way to evaluate the strength of the traders present at the level. Figure 12 illustrates a case where prices bounced after a strong bearish move. Also, notice how they react in the future as prices moved back towards the same level over the next 6 months.

Figure 12: A Strong Swing Point in SPY (Source: TradingView)

Ranges

Ranges are periods of sideways movement in a chart, and they also provide clear indications of support and resistance levels being present. The top and bottom of ranges are areas where many traders reside. Prices usually retest these tops and bottoms repeatedly, and this only reinforces the strength of these levels. Figure 13 illustrates how powerful they can be.

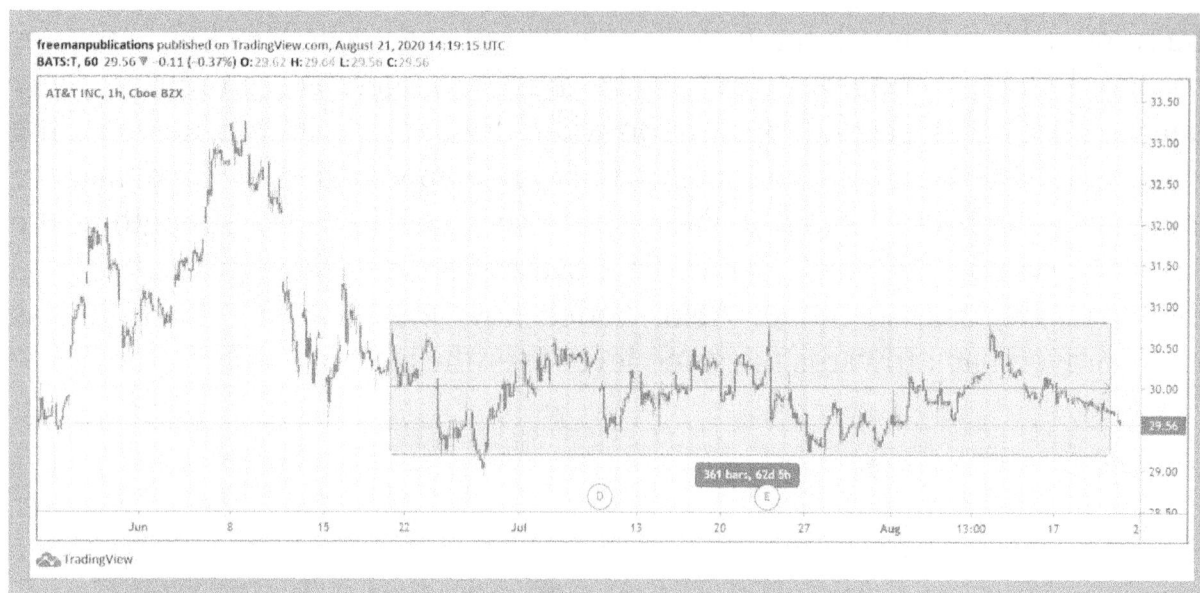

Figure 13: A Range in AT&T (Source: TradingView)

Except for one overnight anomaly, AT&T traded between $29.22 and $30.84 for 62 straight trading days between June 21 and August 17, 2020, making it a perfect candidate for both call and put credit spreads. The reason for this is the presence of strong support and resistance levels at the bottom and top of the range, respectively. This sort of price action is ideal for trading credit spreads.

Figure 13 also contains a number of swing points that act as strong support and resistance. Notice that these points by themselves don't offer much insight as to what the market is doing. In fact, swing point support and resistance levels usually form in trends. If you see a high number of support and resistance levels that are swing points, notice the length of the reactions from these levels.

In Figure 13, notice that AT&T plummeted and gapped down initially on June 10th. The swing points that it printed were small, which indicates that counter trend traders weren't present in huge numbers. This means the chances of a balanced market forming anytime soon were remote. After the gap, the stock's behavior changes. Swing points produce larger reactions, which means the buyers (counter trend traders) are stepping into the market.

At this stage you should be on the lookout for possible sideways movement forming. This eventually comes to pass as AT&T prints a clean range that you could have traded successfully for over two months. Using support and resistance in this manner helps you figure out what the order looks like right now and which way it might go. If you see swing points producing smaller counter trend reactions, it's a sign that the trend traders are getting stronger and that this environment is unsuited for our strategies.

Look for support and resistance ranges to be as stable as possible. There will be unclean price action, and that violates clean, horizontally drawn lines. Remember that support and resistance areas are zones, not single lines. The more unclean a range is, the wider your zone must be and, consequently, the more conservative your strike prices must be.

In the case of AT&T, an ideal short strike for a call spread would have been $31 (slightly above resistance) and an ideal short strike for a put spread would have been $29 (slightly below support).

Moving Averages

When trading credit spreads, we want a market that is either sideways or mildly trending. This is where the price to Exponential Moving Average (EMA) crossover system works perfectly. For bull put spreads we suggest using the 50EMA because it is the most common and available on all free charting tools and trading platforms. This is where a stock's short term (50 day) moving average crosses over its long term (200 day) moving average. This is also known as the "golden cross".

We base this choice on the results obtained during a backtest of this strategy. This backtest on SPY options between 2009 and 2019 sold 0.31 delta put spreads with 30 days to expiry, every time SPY crossed above the 50-day moving average. Using this simple system, you would have made 433% profits over the 10-year period, with a 90.5% win rate across 211 trades, provided you took profits at the 50% mark (losing trades were run to max loss).

Interestingly enough, if you pull the backtest further to include the 2007-2009 bear market, the strategy still provided net positive returns across 46 trades, because it managed to capture some of the market rallies.

This is an extremely simple system to follow and it works very well for a number of reasons. The biggest reason is that it is based on common sense.

Any stock that is crossing its 50EMA is bullish in the short term, but it isn't so bullish so as to overwhelm our strategies. The stock might indeed become extremely bullish over time, but that's a risk we'll have to take in the markets when trading.

For the most part, the 50EMA crossover will highlight stocks that have broken out of a long period of sideways ranging and are beginning to establish some sort of bullishness. If you were to analyze the charts of these stocks and use support and resistance as well, you'd be able to narrow down your prospects better.

If the stock is far too bullish, you can still make money on a bull put spread. However, you will have to deal with increased volatility. Due to volatility increasing, you'll be selling options when they're cheaper and hoping that volatility doesn't grow too much so as to inflate their prices. If the trade goes against you, covering your shorts will result in a loss in this scenario.

This doesn't mean you should not take the trade at all. It's just that you need to be careful. Use the EMA crossover system we just highlighted to create a watchlist and then drill down deeper to look at whether setting up a spread in that stock makes sense.

Bollinger Bands

Bollinger bands are a great trading tool for credit spread traders. Interpreting them is also simple and this makes them a popular tool with directional traders too. From a net credit spread perspective, Bollinger Bands give us clear insight into the state of the underlying stock's volatility.

The bands are plotted at two standard deviations away from the current price. Why two standard deviations? This is because stocks have a 95% probability of trading within this band. If these percentages seem arbitrary, remember how IV levels show the stock having a 68.1% chance of trading within a range; well that's because 68.1% is one standard deviation. As a handy cheat sheet, remember that

- 1 standard deviation = 68.1% chance of being within the range
- 2 standard deviations = 95% chance of being within the range
- 3 standard deviations = 99% chance of being within the range

Bollinger Bands (2 standard deviations, 95% chance) gives us a great way of looking at how volatility changes.

Figure 14 below illustrates what Bollinger Bands look like on a chart.

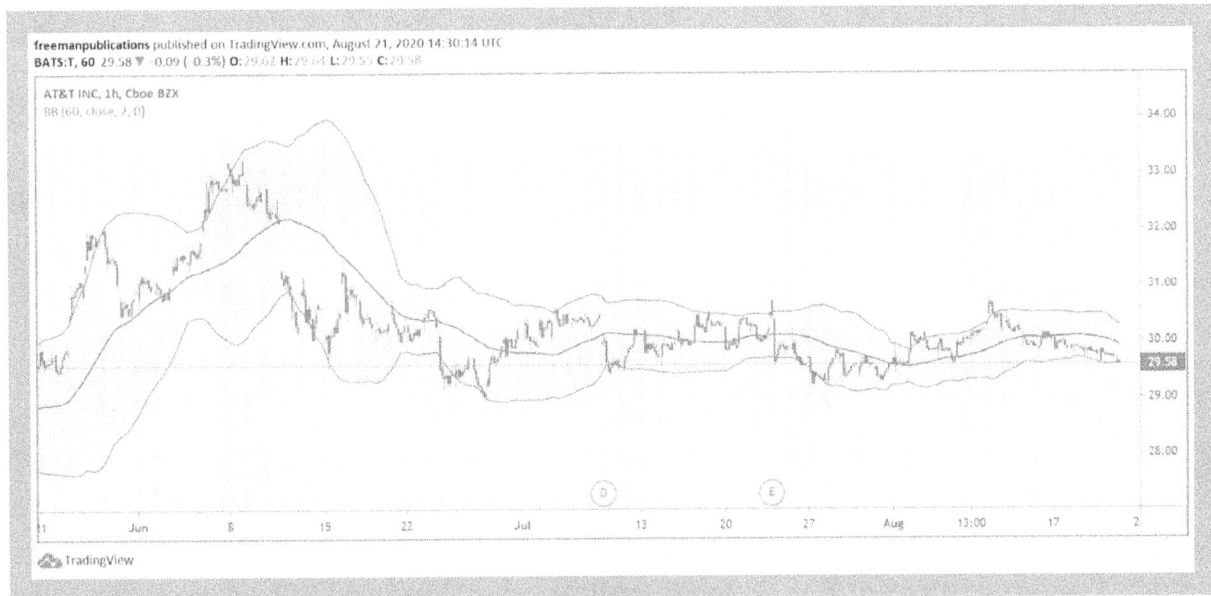

Figure 14: Bollinger Bands in AT&T (Source: TradingView)

The bands above and below price represent two standard deviations' worth of movement. The line through the center of price is the EMA. In Figure 14, we've chosen the 60-day EMA, so this represents around three months' worth of price action (because 60 trading days = 3 months real time). 60-day EMA is a stable line that isn't going to fluctuate too much.

Notice that prices rarely peek out above the bands. The minute they do so, a swift regression to the mean follows. In some cases, it's immediate, while in others, it takes more time. Notice that during powerful trends, AT&T takes a while to get back within the band envelope. It's easy to think that all you'll need to do with Bollinger Bands is to look at when the stock peeks out below or above the bands and bet on it moving in the opposite direction. This is what directional traders do.

However, for credit spreads, we like to have 30 to 45-day trade timelines. The underlying could move in the opposite direction for a short time and then reverse and continue in its original path. For example, notice the trending sections of AT&T in Figure 14.

For the purpose of credit spreads, instead of focusing on whether the stock is near the edge of the band, look at the width of the bands themselves. Notice in the trending portion of Figure 14, the bands widen massively. This indicates that IV of the underlying is increasing massively. Since we're looking for low volatility conditions, it's obvious that we need to stay away from this stock. Ideal conditions for credit spreads are when the bands are beginning to contract.

In Figure 14, notice how the upper band collapses to meet the lower band once the trend ends and as AT&T settles into a range. The tighter a range gets, the better it is for you as an options seller. It means volatility is lower and you can sell closer to the money options and capture higher premiums. Be careful of bands that are too constricted, though.

The bands often act as springs. If they get wound too tight, they're likely to explode outwards. Prolonged ranges tend to produce this effect. This stands to reason from an order flow perspective. In large ranges, traders redistribute their holdings and seek to push prices in their preferred direction once this is done. Towards the end of a large range you'll notice bar sizes reducing dramatically and higher lows or lower highs forming. This indicates that the stock is getting ready to move explosively in a given direction and begin a new trend. The bands will have been squeezed tight, to the extent that they'll constrict prices completely. Compare the relative band widths over the past 30-60 days to figure out whether you should be on the lookout for a new trend.

In Figure 14, notice how the bands come extremely close and how the price bars reduce in size dramatically. Compare the width of the bands and the bar sizes to those on the left. Since prices are below the 60EMA, we would hazard a guess that AT&T is looking to break out into a bearish trend. If we had any open bullish positions at this point, we'd wind them up and set up bear call spreads.

A bear call spread is not the most efficient setup for a high volatility environment, but this doesn't mean it's an incorrect setup. We'll still make money on it. We just won't make as much money as we could with other setups. Our point is that the bands have given us plenty of notice of the new trend possibly forming and we can take full advantage of this.

This closes our look at technical analysis indicators. Hopefully, this reassures you that you don't need to know every indicator or chart pattern under the sun to get started. By focusing on the basics like support and resistance levels, Bollinger bands, and identifying ranges, you will confidently identify good candidates for credit spreads.

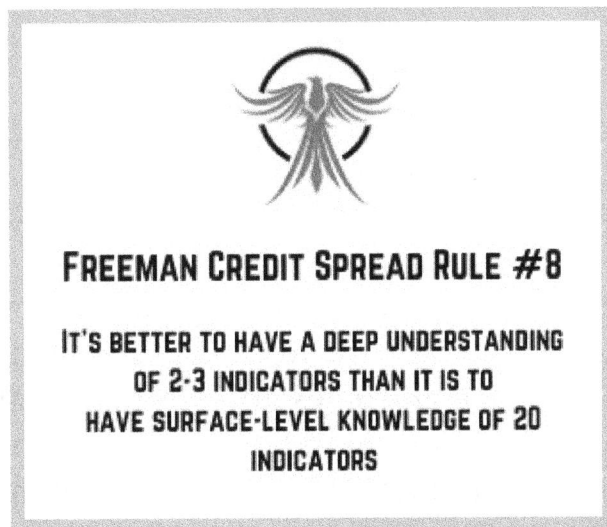

FREEMAN CREDIT SPREAD RULE #8

IT'S BETTER TO HAVE A DEEP UNDERSTANDING
OF 2-3 INDICATORS THAN IT IS TO
HAVE SURFACE-LEVEL KNOWLEDGE OF 20
INDICATORS

If you're entirely new to credit spreads or stock charts, here is a useful practice exercise. Go to tradingview.com (you can open an account for free) and find the charts for 5-10 stocks you are interested in. Practice drawing support and resistance lines on these and identify whether the stock is trending or trading within a range. Feel free to share your results and interpretations with us. If you get stuck, you can email us at admin@ freemanpublications.com and we'll help you out.

CHOOSING THE RIGHT INSTRUMENTS TO TRADE

The best strategies need great instruments. Without the right instruments, you will struggle to capture the highest gains a strategy can give you. When it comes to selecting instruments for credit spreads, we need to return to our investment criteria. These three strategies work best when volatility is low. Which by itself eliminates a lot of the possible candidates you can trade.

Mildly bullish or mildly bearish conditions are ideal for these setups, which you can use the technical indicators you learned in the last chapter to identify. This immediately eliminates strong trending stocks since they tend to be extremely volatile.

While the broad market has periods where it trends sideways, don't mistake overall market behavior for individual instrument behavior. For example, at the time of writing the S&P 500 is up around four percent this year (2020). While the NASDAQ is up 27%. The energy sector (as represented by the XLE ETF) meanwhile is down 37%.

This shows that every sector and stock has its own rhythms, so it's possible to find bearish conditions even in extremely bullish market environments. When it comes to writing credit spreads, you have three types of instruments to choose from, let's take a look at them one by one.

INDEX OPTIONS

The safest choice for beginners is an index option. You can trade options on broad market indexes, or you can choose sector indexes. The best indexes to focus on are the SPX (which covers the S&P 500) and RUT (which covers the Russell 2000). You can also trade the ETFs connected to these indexes. We'll discuss ETFs in the next section in this chapter. Many sector indexes don't have options tied to them, so you'll have to stick to trading their ETFs.

Index options are different from their individual stock and ETF option counterparts because, unlike the latter, these options don't cover a tradable instrument. After all, you can't buy the SPX or RUT no matter how hard you try. This means their options are cash settled. When you buy the options, you'll receive or pay the equivalent cash that the underlying movements will create.

For example, if your options finish ITM and you're assigned them, you won't have to buy the SPX. Instead, your broker will charge you whatever amount your trade will cause you to pay. You can't own the underlying as you can with other instruments. Cash-settled options are great if you're more conservative because you automatically avoid assignment fees and don't have to worry about them being exercised by the buyer.

If you find a broker that is great but charges assignment fees, you can trade cash-settled index options with them and avoid the fee completely. Take note that cash-settled options exist on a number of instruments other than just indexes. Commodity indexes and futures contract options are cash-settled, as are precious metal spot contract options.

Stick to broad market or large sector indexes since these will witness a good amount of liquidity, and you won't be caught out by unexpected volatility. Thinly traded index options are ripe for manipulation. This happens through wide spreads, so watch out for them. As a rule, the greater the liquidity is in an instrument, the closer its spread will be.

ETFS

ETFs, or exchange traded funds, are an extremely popular trading instrument since they accurately represent sector performance. ETFs have been growing in recognition since the last financial crisis. In fact, total assets under management in the entire ETF industry has gone from $534 Billion in 2008, to more than $3.4 Trillion in 2018. As a result, there is an ETF for pretty much everything now. ETFs also tend to be far more liquid than individual stocks while also providing liquidity for traders looking to speculate in obscure indexes.

For example, if you wanted to speculate on the price of gold, trading the spot option contracts would put you in a precarious position. This is because they're not the most liquid of instruments. However, by trading the options on a gold ETF you can speculate on gold's price without having to put yourself at the risk of holding onto an illiquid position. The most popular ETF for options speculation purpose is SPY. SPY and SPX options attract a lot of interest but are different. SPX options are cash-settled, as you just learned. SPY is not cash-settled and upon exercise, you'll end up owning shares of the ETF.

This means you'll pay assignment fees. There isn't much of a difference other than settlement when it comes to trading the SPX versus SPY. SPY tracks the SPX, so you'll end up gaining and losing the same amount. You might find some discrepancies in pricing for the same strike level between the two option chains, but largely the options trade for similar premiums.

There are other notable ETFs that offer great trading opportunities. IWM is the most liquid ETF, which tracks the Russell 2000 Index while QQQ tracks the NASDAQ 100 index. XLV is a popular ETF to trade if you're looking to take advantage of movements in the healthcare sector. XMB (materials), XLF (financials), XLE (energy) and VWO (emerging markets) are other popular options.

When choosing an ETF, liquidity should be your primary concern. Liquidity can be easily measured by looking at the size of the ETF. The larger it is, the more liquid it will be. There are many obscure ETFs that track similar indexes to the bigger ones, but they don't attract as much investor attention. This means their shares are not as liquid, which in turn means their options are even less liquid and spreads may widen at any time.

ETFs are a speculation tool as well. This is done through leveraged and inverse ETFs. If you want to boost your returns or profit from a drop in index values, these ETFs can provide you with that sort of exposure. However, for the purposes of net credit spread trading, they're a poor choice. This is because their volatility is inherently high. The second reason is that in periods of serious price movement, they are often suspended from trading and this throws their options all over the place.

These ETFs utilize large amounts of leverage to generate their returns, and this is why volatility is high. When trading options, you'll be leveraging your investment to a certain extent. After all, you'll be buying one contract and controlling 100 shares. To further leverage your investment by choosing a leveraged ETF is a poor choice.

Pay special attention to the trading volumes of the ETFs you choose. At the very least, stick to ETFs that have more than 500,000 shares traded every day. This will guarantee liquidity at all times. Size is a good proxy for liquidity as we mentioned earlier. You can look for any ETF that has at least five billion dollars under management. Anything below this is risky.

The prices of an ETF's options also depend on how well the manager runs the fund. Many smaller ETFs tend to be volatile because their managers are unproven. The slightest hint of trouble could lead to investors selling their units in the fund, causing its price to drop. An option holder is exposed to such price drops as well as sector performance. This is why it's best to stick to proven ETFs issued by larger companies like Vanguard, State Street and iShares by BlackRock.

INDIVIDUAL STOCKS

Individual stocks are where you'll find the most candidates for setting up net credit spread trades. The big stocks such as Apple and Google (Alphabet) are quite liquid and stable for the most part in terms of volatility. The criteria regarding liquidity applies to stocks as well. However, the size of a company isn't a proxy for its liquidity. Look at just the number of shares traded (more than 500,000 shares per day) to determine this.

Stay away from the media darlings or any stock that is being targeted by activist firms. Activist firms are usually hedge funds or private equity firms who buy controlling stakes in companies and try to force changes in their operations. Their results could be hit-or-miss, but what is guaranteed is a power struggle.

If you read news of the stock in the media, this is a good sign that it's best to stay away from it. A good example of this in the current market are stocks of Electric Vehicle companies. Everyone is jumping into these companies like there's no tomorrow despite the fact that most of them cannot profitably make cars (and for some, even generate any revenue at all). Meaning they are extremely volatile and make for poor credit spread candidates. Remember, you can use IV levels to measure this. An IV of greater than 50% is a sign you should stay away from the stock.

If you need a starting point for potential candidates, you can use free stock screeners to select appropriate stocks. We prefer using FinViz.com for this because it's free and easy to use.

We have a free Finviz tutorial on our YouTube channel, which you can find at https://freemanpublications.com/youtube

Here are the criteria we recommend:

- Stocks trading above 50-day moving average criteria
- Trading Volume > 500k shares per day
- Optionable
- Mid and large cap stocks only

- Earnings announcement in the previous week

All of these criteria fulfill certain requirements. A stock that is trading above its 50-day EMA gives us a list of stocks that can satisfy our bull put spread backtest criteria as we mentioned earlier. Alternatively, you could set up a screen that alerts you to crossovers. The trading volume criteria is so we have enough liquidity to get the best prices.

By limiting yourself to mid and large cap stocks you're insulating yourself from volatility by a large extent. Small cap stocks and stocks that are priced under $10 tend to be extremely volatile since they attract the penny stock trading crowd. Small caps also face greater headwinds in terms of business challenges, so their stock prices tend to fluctuate much more than a larger company's stock does.

Running the above scan on FinViz at the time of writing gave us 52 possible candidates, including well-known names like Barrick Gold, Draftkings, Applied Materials, Inc. and Marriott. If you have a smaller account or are only looking for stocks less than $50, 31 companies fit these criteria.

Stocks and Instruments to Stay Away From

We've told you what to choose, so it's best for us to explicitly tell you which instruments to stay away from. Here are the criteria for these:

- Instruments which don't directly track stock prices (USO)
- Inverse ETFs in which trading can be halted (SEF)
- Instruments directly related to volatility levels (UVXY)
- Leveraged ETFs (TQQQ, DWT, DUST)
- Media darlings or stocks receiving a lot of attention (NKLA, TSLA, KODK, MRNA)

All of these instruments are volatility magnets, so stay away from them. Especially, UVXY which is an ETF that tracks the short-term futures of the VIX. Volatility tends to stay relatively flat, but every now and then, it spikes massively, meaning it can throw a trade from almost certainty profitability to maximum loss in the space of a few hours.

FREEMAN CREDIT SPREAD RULE #9

STICK TO TRADING CREDIT SPREADS ON STOCK, INDEX AND LARGE ETF OPTIONS

Beyond these criteria, you don't need any other specific tool to trade credit spreads well, but one particular indicator you can add is the Choppiness Index.

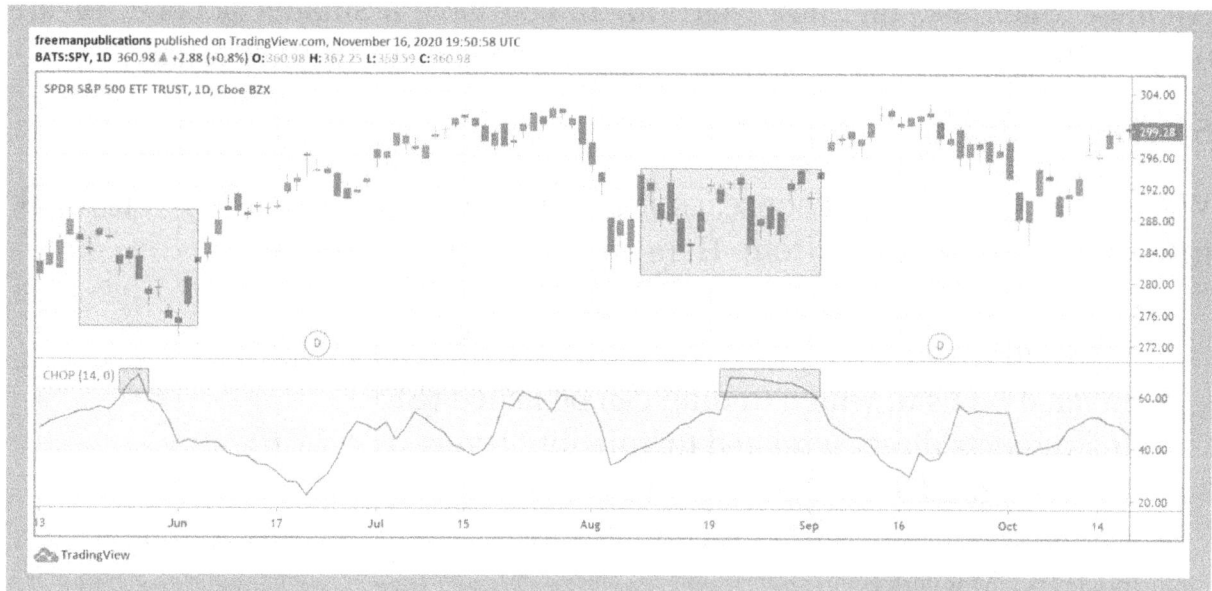

Figure 15: Choppiness Index on SPY (Source: TradingView)

This indicator measures the ranging character of the markets. Values greater than 61.8 (look, it's our old friend 61.8 again) are considered indicative of a range. As you can see from Figure 15, once the indicator passes 61.8 it correctly manages to predict the existence of two ranges in the SPY ETF. The range on the left is smaller, and you can see the larger range on the right.

Once again, you don't have to use this indicator; it's merely our suggestion. However, if you find the previous chapter's indicators aren't helping you too much, then layering the Choppiness Index is a good idea.

At this point, you might be wondering if it's best to trade index options, ETFs or stock options? There is no such thing as the "best" when it comes to credit spread trading.

Indexes are far less volatile than individual stocks, so you might find that it's easier to score a high number of wins with them. However, their lower volatility means their premiums won't be mispriced, so your overall profits might be lower. If you trade cash-settled options, you'll avoid assignment fees, which can boost your profit as well. Individual stocks are more volatile, and this creates more opportunities for mispricing in their options. You'll earn a greater profit per trade, but your win rate might be lower due to additional volatility.

Try out all instrument types before choosing to stick with one type of instrument. Then choose the one that suits you the best or find the easiest to consistently win with. It's important to remember that you can make large profits by trading the same instrument over and over again. In our experience, beginners tend to prefer index options like SPX or RUT.

10

SELECTING THE RIGHT STRIKE PRICES

Your choice of strike prices directly affects the profitability of your trades. Selecting the right strike prices is tricky because you want to be close enough to the money that you'll earn a significant profit, but you also want to be far enough away from prices so that your options finish OTM. When we highlighted the strategies in detail in an earlier chapter, we first mentioned that the short option legs will begin ITM and finish OTM.

This kind of a trade setup will bring in huge premiums since ITM options will be priced higher than OTM ones. We then mentioned that if you wish to minimize the risk of early assignment, you ought to write further OTM options. This reduces the premium you'll receive, but the probability of winning the trade is much higher. There's also zero risk of early assignment because both legs will be OTM.

There's no clear-cut method of determining the right strike price every time. A lot depends on your own risk profile. If you're someone who doesn't mind losing more to make more money, then writing ITM options might make sense to you. Many people justify the increased risk through the higher premiums earned. Figure 16 illustrates why this is.

Figure 16 shows the option prices for two spreads on Disney. Disney was trading at $211.50 at the time we took the screen capture. The options listed are calls.

We have two choices for a $5 wide spread. We can either select the 220-215 or 235-230 strikes for our bear call spread. Since the 215 call is closest to the money, you can see that it has the highest premium. However, the 220 call is also more expensive.

Our net credit from this pair of strikes will be $1.77 per share (5.07 – 3.30) or $177 per contract. Our maximum risk will be the difference between the strike prices minus the premium earned. This is $323 per contract, giving us a risk/reward ratio of 54.7%

In the case of the second spread, our premium earned will be $0.46 per share (1.29 – 0.83) or $46 per contract. Our risk will be $454, giving us a risk/reward ratio of 10.1%.

As you can see, the differences in profit versus loss amounts are large for both spreads. The former spread brings us a larger premium of $177 per contract, but the trade itself has a higher probability of a loss. The second spread brings us a far lower premium, and the maximum loss is also higher than the former. However, there's a higher probability the trade itself will be a winner. As you can see, there's no one-size-fits-all answer to this.

What we can do is reverse-engineer the process. To do this, we start with avoiding loss, which begins with the probability of the trade finishing ITM. If you wish to avoid losing money, the amount of premium you can earn should be of no consequence. As long as you're earning a decent amount of money, focus solely on the probability of the win. To do this, stick to writing further OTM options.

Even if you don't mind running additional risks, it is our view that capturing steady and more probable gains is a better strategy than chasing individual wins. You will earn more on individual trades, but over time the probabilities will assert themselves, and you're not going to gain too much of an advantage over someone who writes further OTM spreads. The latter method also has the advantage of being far more comfortable to implement mentally since you don't need the market to do anything other than remain where it is.

Market conditions also play an important role. If you feel that a move in the markets is almost certain to occur, you can write ITM options and wait for the move to take place. However, keep in mind that you'll still be running more considerable risks of loss in such a trade.

Before entering any trade, it's best to fix a few worst-case scenario exit points. For example, from the scenario in Figure 16, if we wrote the 215 option, we could have fixed $218 as the highest we would tolerate the stock moving. This is lower than our maximum risk point of 220 and it reduces our loss significantly. If we were aware of the increased risk we were running in this trade, fixing such exit points ahead of time in our minds is a good choice.

Of course, there is the chance that Disney might move to 219 and then fall back down to 205, in which case we would have exited the trade too quickly. However, these kinds of risks are calculated business risks you'll need to take if you wish to trade.

There is no way you'll ever select the perfect strike price every single time, so don't try to do so. Instead, focus on the probability of loss and work from there, minimizing it at every step but not minimizing it to the extent that you earn an extremely small amount of money.

Always begin by selecting your short strike first. This is what earns you money on your trade, so fix this level before moving on to selecting your long strike. It's best to keep the long option within 1-2 strikes of your short option to minimize risk. This will result in less wiggle room for your trade, but it will cap your risk significantly.

If you're going to write ITM options, it's best to buy an option that is one strike away. This will make it easy for you to decide whether you wish to remain in the trade or not. Once you gain more experience, you can play around with selecting strikes that are further away. A long strike that is deeply OTM gives your trade more opportunity to move against you and while also having more leeway to move in the direction that benefits you. Such reversals occur all the time, but the odds of a beginner finding such instances are low. Usually, if the trade moves against you and stays against you for over 15 days, it's probably going to go for a loss.

This assumes you stick to our recommended 30 to 45-day holding period. A 15-day losing period means half the time your trade has been open; it would have resulted in a loss for you. The odds of it suddenly moving into profit are low, especially if volatility is decreasing. Let's move on and see how technical analysis can help us.

USING TECHNICAL ANALYSIS TO DETERMINE STRIKE PRICES

Technical analysis offers us an easy way to determine strike prices. Support and resistance levels are obvious regions for placing our short calls. In the case of a bull put spread, it's best to place the short strike slightly below a support level. This will give the setup additional protection against unexpected bearish swings. The presence of the support level, and the traders that come with it, will ensure that a move below this level will be potentially short-lived.

Similarly, placing the short strike above a resistance level in the case of a bear call spread will offer you added protection. Take care to notice how clean the support or resistance level is. Levels are rarely clean enough for you to draw a perfect horizontal line through them. In most cases you'll find that the market hangs around in a zone. Your degree of aggressiveness determines how deep or shallow within the zone you wish to place yourself. For example, in a bull put spread, you could choose to place the short strike at a shallow level in the support zone. This will increase your premium earned but makes the option finishing ITM more likely.

A strike that is deep within support will earn you less money, but it's more likely to finish OTM. When choosing where to place the short strike, take a look at the price distribution within the zone. Areas where price regularly retreats to within the zone or areas where it bounces away from are where most traders are present. You should look to place yourself at the extremities of these areas. You'll find that these areas get redistributed in large ranges and that the new support and resistance levels might have to be redrawn.

If the idea of using technical analysis to find the best strike prices overwhelms you, then our next method may be more up your street.

USING DELTA TO DETERMINE STRIKE PRICES

We discussed earlier that an option's delta serves as a proxy for determining how likely it is to finish ITM. This means we can also use delta to determine levels at which to place our strikes, which is the methodology we taught in our book *Covered Calls for Beginners*.

A delta of 0.16 (which is a proxy for that strike price having 16% chance of finishing ITM) is one standard deviation away from the current price. This is an important number to note because it plays an important part in determining where to place your strikes.

A backtest carried out by *projectoption* tested bull put spreads on the SPY from 2008-2020 (projectoption, 2020). In this test, the participant sold puts with deltas of 0.3, two standard deviations away from price, and bought puts of 0.16 delta. The positions were entered on the first day of the month and exited on the month's final day, regardless of profitability. This strategy yielded a 74% chance of the trader having their options finishing OTM.

Note that put deltas are negative, and we've quoted positive numbers here. When speaking of put deltas, it's important to focus on the absolute value and ignore the sign. Put deltas move just like call deltas do, so the sign is irrelevant here.

This backtest highlights how deltas play an essential part in option strike prices. Combine this with support and resistance levels, and you'll manage to build pretty high probabilities into your trade working out in your favor.

Other Factors to Note when Entering Your Order

When entering your orders, you'll have the option to enter at the market rate or on limit. We usually advise entering a limit order in the middle of the spread. Heavily traded instruments generally have lower spreads, and this makes it possible to achieve a middle of the spread fill. For example, the SPY sometimes witnesses spreads as low as $0.05 for ITM options. Even one of the most heavily traded stocks such as Google has spreads as wide as $0.80 for ITM options. This is on the lower end for stocks but doesn't compare to the SPY.

However, not all indexes witness low spreads. For example, RUT options sometimes have spreads as wide as $1.50. Using a market order on such wide spreads is inadvisable since it might result in you receiving poor order fills, which makes profitability tough. Be patient, target the middle of the spread to enter trades, and never chase a trade if it moves past your ideal entry point.

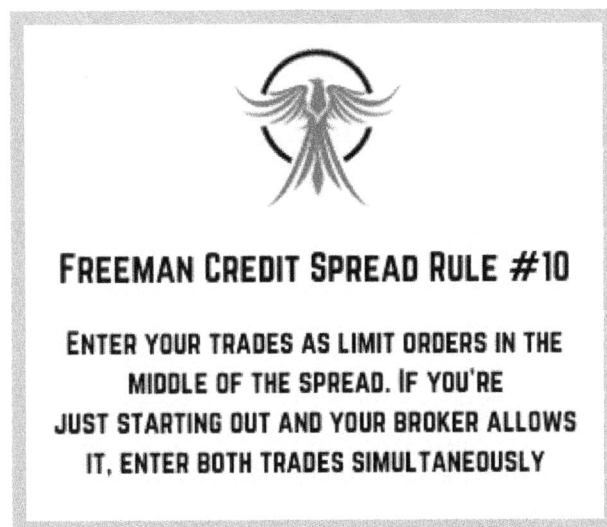

FREEMAN CREDIT SPREAD RULE #10

ENTER YOUR TRADES AS LIMIT ORDERS IN THE
MIDDLE OF THE SPREAD. IF YOU'RE
JUST STARTING OUT AND YOUR BROKER ALLOWS
IT, ENTER BOTH TRADES SIMULTANEOUSLY

Another point to note with price is that you'll find it tough to enter all 4 legs of an Iron Butterfly at once with some brokers. This usually happens with brokers who aren't well-versed with offering options trading services. An experienced broker will let you enter all four legs at once, and you'll receive quick fills. If your broker doesn't let you do this, enter both spreads separately.

This means you'll enter the bull spread and then the bear spread. Don't mix the legs together and enter short before entering long or vice versa. This will trigger all kinds of risk limit violations on your broker's side and they'll shut you down quickly.

Speaking of trade entry points, we have one final secret weapon that gives you an advantage in knowing if you should enter a trade or not.

11

YOUR SECRET WEAPON FOR TRADE ENTRY - THE VIX

Volatility can be both your best friend and your worst enemy. Many struggling options traders label volatility as being the "best" or the "worst" and use such extreme language to talk about it. In truth, volatility is what you make of it. You can't influence it, so it's best to try to stick to its good side. With respect to credit spread trades, you want to operate in low volatility environments, with the ideal environment being one where volatility is decreasing.

Many inexperienced options sellers chase high volatility environments for two reasons. The first is due to a hangover from directional trading. In that world, volatility is needed for a directional trader to make money, because they can't earn anything if the market moves sideways, so they root for highly volatile market conditions. If you're trading net credit spreads, this isn't what you want.

This brings us to the second reason for chasing high volatility conditions. Option premiums tend to be overpriced during such times, and the prospect of earning high premiums can push traders to choose to write ITM or ATM options. The increased volatility means that the difference in premiums between ATM and OTM options tends to be larger than in normal times. This creates a further incentive for people to push their luck writing ITM options.

Instead of trying to guess where they need to write options, such traders would be better served by analyzing the overall market's volatility. This is especially the case if they're operating in index options. The market's volatility is measured by the volatility index or the VIX.

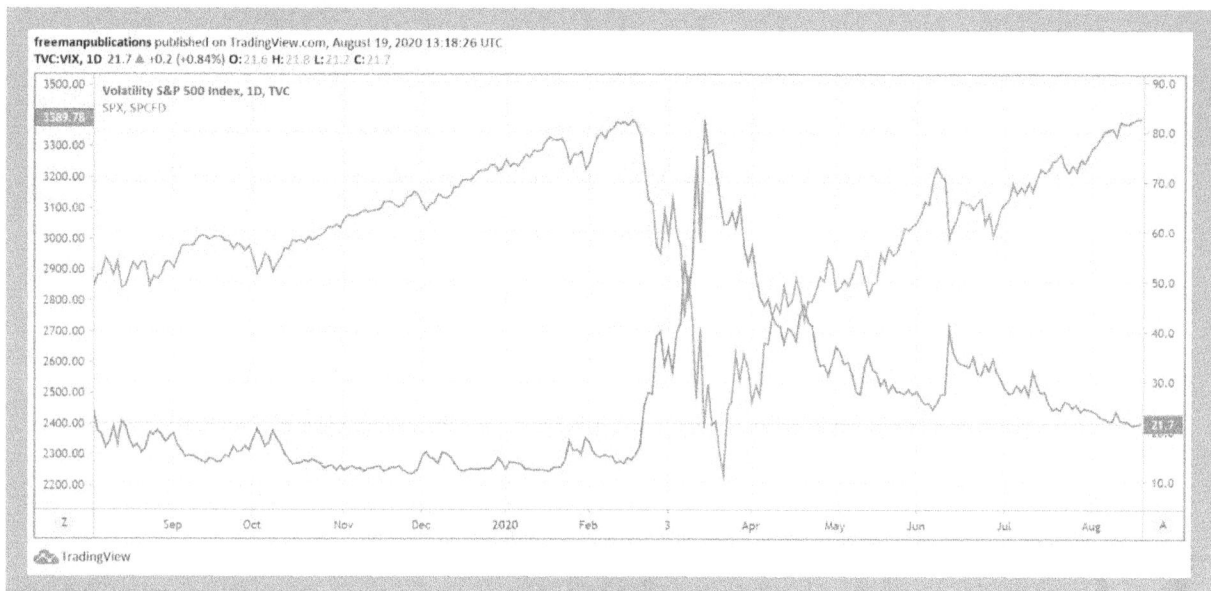

Figure 17: The Correlation Between the VIX and the S&P 500 from Aug 2019 to Aug 2020 (Source: TradingView)

Figure 17 illustrates the correlation between the VIX and the S&P 500 for a 12-month period, beginning in August 2019. As you can see, the VIX starts off low on the left of the chart and then spikes massively as the COVID-related market drop occurred. On March 18th 2020, the VIX closed at 82.69, the highest level since October 2008. Once the market settled down and began climbing again, the VIX fell back to lower levels, even though the numbers are higher than they were in 2019.

Think of the VIX as being the slope of the S&P 500's curve. The sharper the moves in the S&P 500 are, the higher the VIX will be. From a net credit spread perspective, the ideal scenario is to take advantage of high volatility to low volatility transitional periods. The entire period since the market drop has presented such a scenario. However, you need to take the levels of the VIX into account as well.

In the previous chapter, we highlighted a backtest of S&P 500 options that resulted in a 74% win rate. If we were to eliminate entering trades when the VIX was greater than 30, our win rate rises to 77% in that same backtest. A three percent bump doesn't sound like much, but under these conditions, the strategies' overall profitability increases by 50%, which is significant. A simple volatility adjustment allows us to earn an additional 50%.

While the VIX is significant when trading index options, it plays an important role in individual stocks' movements as well. However, much depends on the nature and quality of the stock. If you're focusing on obscure small cap stocks, the VIX is unlikely to affect it too much.

However, if you're operating on one of the bigger stocks in the S&P 500 index, you can bet that the VIX will affect its option prices. A good example of this are the FAANG stocks (Facebook, Apple, Amazon, Netflix, and Google). These five companies are heavily weighted in the S&P 500 and any movement in their stock impacts the overall index.

For this reason, it's best to enter trades in these stocks only when the VIX is below 30. This will ensure the odds of a win are on your side and that any sudden moves won't catch you out. It's impossible to predict what might cause the market to move, of course. However, instead of focusing on predicting market movements, it's best to focus on stacking the odds in our favor as much as possible.

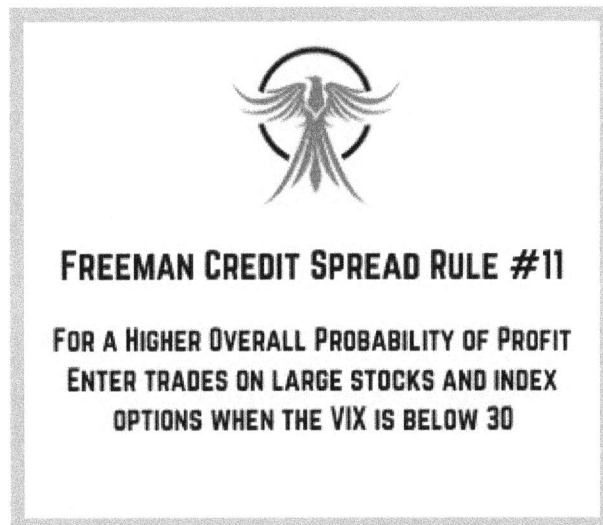

FREEMAN CREDIT SPREAD RULE #11

FOR A HIGHER OVERALL PROBABILITY OF PROFIT ENTER TRADES ON LARGE STOCKS AND INDEX OPTIONS WHEN THE VIX IS BELOW 30

We've already mentioned that you need to stay away from trading options on the VIX itself. This is a bet on volatility and is an extremely risky one. On the surface, it seems like a decent trade because the VIX doesn't spike very often. However, volatility and the VIX is a derivative of the market's movement. Which means writing options on the VIX is creating a derivative of a derivative. It's not an intuitive way to trade, and it can go wrong for you in a hurry. For this reason, stick to stock and index options.

Now we've determined the ideal time to enter trades, let's talk about how you can manage them once they are live.

12

TRADE MANAGEMENT - EASIER THAN YOU THINK

T rade management is a tricky thing to get right. You shouldn't set and forget your trades ever, but the good news is that you also don't need to remain present in front of your screen the entire time.

There are different ways of managing a trade, but to make things simple, we will focus on setting appropriate take profit and stop loss levels.

We'll begin by first looking at our previously cited backtest of bull put spreads between 2008 to 2020 by *projectoption*. In the previous chapter, we ascertained that by waiting until the VIX was below 30 before entering, the strategy's overall profitability increased by 50%.

The backtesters also added a few trade management variables to their base test, which produced some interesting results.

They tested different trade management options by implementing three take profit levels. These were set at 25% of the maximum profits as well as 50% and 75%. Which meant as soon as the trade reached 25% (or 50 or 75%) of its maximum potential profit, it was immediately closed out. This captured the profits at that level, regardless of how long the options had until expiry.

The 25% level had the highest win rate, winning 86% of all trades. However, it also had the lowest overall profitability. This is because the win amounts were so low that all it took was a single loss to cancel these out. The longer the trades ran, the higher overall profits were captured. The 75% take profit level had the lowest win rate at 76%, but it had the highest overall profit at the end of the backtest.

While this deals with take profit levels, what of stop losses? After all, stop losses are what protect you from capturing a loss. The approach *projectoption* implemented was quite novel. Remember that the way we are setting up our trades, the maximum loss is much larger than the maximum profit. To help mitigate this risk, stop losses were set at -100% gains.

When the trade moved into a position where the loss was equal to the maximum gain, it was closed out. Note that we're talking about the negative value of the maximum gain and not the maximum loss. With this strategy, we're eliminating the maximum loss from the picture with our trades.

For example, if the maximum profit was $300 and the maximum loss was $900, the trade would be closed out if the loss reached $300. Higher stop loss levels of -200% and -300% were also tested in the backtest, but these didn't yield greater overall profits.

This backtest's net result is that as a new trader, you can quickly see that micromanaging your trades isn't going to give you greater gains. In fact, you'll be overcomplicating your trades. It's best to establish sensible rules such as these that have been validated by backtests and then trade according to them.

The approach that will result in the least hassle is taking profits at 75% of maximum profits and setting up a stop loss equal to 100% of your maximum profit. This rules-based approach will help you automate your trade management to a great degree.

SETTING UP LEVELS IN YOUR TRADING ACCOUNT

Now that we've explained how we prefer setting up stop loss and take profit targets let's look at how we input these in your brokerage account. A protective stop order for an option credit spread can be established with the "trigger" for the stop being either:

1. The net premium value of the spread itself
2. The price of the underlying stock, index or ETF

The easiest way to set this up is always to use the first option. That is, to set up our stop loss based on the net premium value of the spread. The important thing to remember is we're using the *net* premium value. This means we have to factor in our initial credit when setting our stop loss order. Let's look at an example to understand this better.

Let's say we enter a $4 wide bull put spread on Oracle (NYSE:ORCL). We sell the 59 put and buy the 55 put for a net credit of $1. For this trade, our max profit is $1, and a max loss is $3 ($4 difference between strike prices - $1 credit on entry.)

Therefore a stop loss equal to -100% of max profit should be set at -$1.

We would then enter a STOP order in our broker platform. In some platforms, this will be listed as a stop order, followed by choosing "market" on the next screen. In other platforms you might simply click "stop market" order as an option.

Note that when we're buying a spread back, we are entering the opposite order to our initial trade. In the ORCL example, this means we are now buying the 59 put and selling the 55 put. This closes out our trade.

Some platforms, like Tastyworks, have a "swap" option, which automatically flips the order. Others will allow you to create a "closing order" or "opposite order" if you select both legs of your spread on the active trades tab.

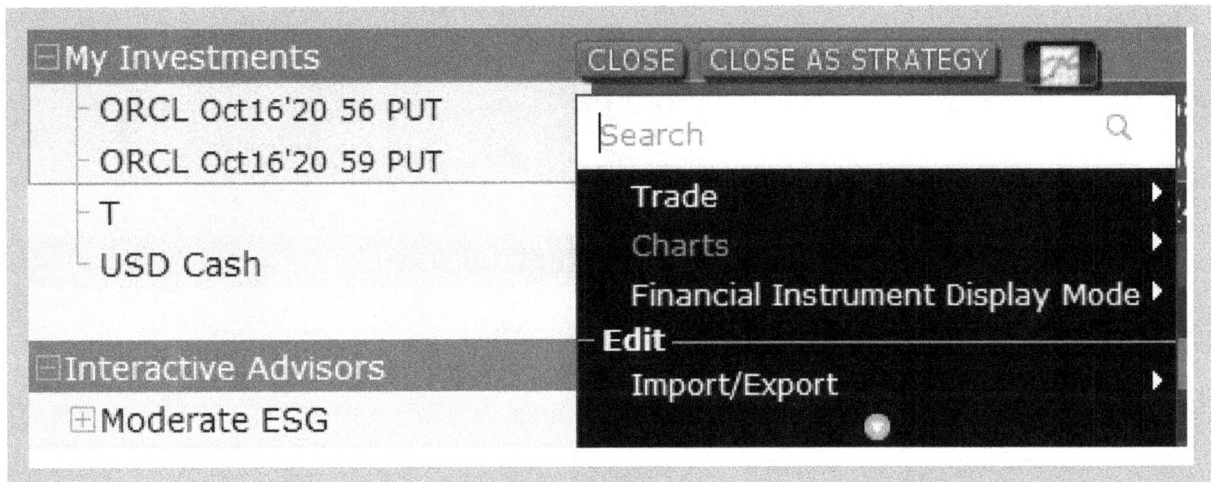

Figure 18: Order Entry Screen in Interactive Brokers

Figure 18 illustrates the order entry screen in Interactive Brokers. Here, you'll select both legs of your spread and right click on it. Click "close" after this, and this closes your spread out.

Keep in mind that you will <u>not</u> enter the order for a $1 value. This will stop us out when our net profit on the trade is $0. We've already received $1 in credit and ($1 - $1) = $0. Always remember that stop orders are triggered by the net premium value of the spread.

Therefore we enter our stop order for $2, because we want to be stopped out when the net premium value of the trade is -$1. To hit -$1 in losses, we need the trade to move $2 against us. Once the trade reaches this -$1 mark, our order will be converted to a market order and automatically executed by our broker.

Make sure you set your stop order as "good until canceled" or GTC, rather than one that expires at the end of the day. This is key because default stop orders in most platforms expire at the end of the day.

Lastly, remember that you will pay commissions for this stop order, so remember to consider your overall P&L calculations.

Setting up Take Profit Levels

Setting up a take profit order is a lot simpler than setting up a stop loss order in most platforms. We simply set a stop order at 75% of whatever our initial credit was since this is the level we wish to exit our trade at. In our ORCL example, our initial credit was $1. This means we set our stop order at $0.75. Note that this stop order refers to your take profit and not your stop loss. It's simply a stop order that causes you to exit for a profit. Figure 19 illustrates what the take profit order setup looks like in Tastyworks.

Figure 19: Setting up a Take Profit Order in Tastyworks

One advantage of Tastyworks is that you can set up your take profit orders based on percentages automatically. This means you don't have to calculate your take profit target yourself.

If some of this sounds confusing, don't worry, we have a number of video explanations for how to set up these orders on our YouTube channel which you can find at https://freemanpublications.com/youtube

Note that every brokerage account has a different layout. If you can't find the exact steps to set your orders up on your broker's website, it's best to call their customer support and have them walk you through the process.

If you're just getting started on a new platform, we recommend first trading using a paper account before jumping into live trading. This will help you become acclimated to how your platform works, and you'll avoid losing money due to fat finger errors or other errors caused by incorrect order entry. These mistakes are far more common than you think, so take care to avoid them.

MANAGING BUTTERFLY SPREADS

Managing Iron Butterflies is a bit more complex than credit spreads. This is because of the way the trade is structured. The sweet spot for an Iron Butterfly is pretty well defined. If the underlying doesn't trade at the exact price at which you wrote your short options, the maximum profit isn't realized. This means we ought to be more prudent with our stop loss and take profit targets.

One method is to ignore the top third of the profit range because of the low probability that the stock will trade in this range at expiry. As a result, we're focused just on the bottom two-thirds of the profit range and we aren't mentally anchored to the max profit level.

The easiest way to manage the trade is to stick to standard take profit and stop loss levels. For Iron Butterflies, these are typically 15% for profits and 25% for max loss. 15% of maximum profits might seem small, but remember Butterflies are structured in such a way that max profit is greater than max loss. This means 15% of the maximum profit is a good target.

There are more proactive ways of managing your trade. We'll only discuss neutral Butterflies for the purposes of this book. The great thing about a neutral Butterfly is that only one side of your trade is typically in danger. After all, if you've constructed a neutral spread the underlying cannot simultaneously be above and below your short strikes. This makes trade management a bit easier.

The rule of thumb for managing Butterfly spreads is to adjust your trade before it reaches break even. Newer traders typically adjust after break even has been breached, and they tend to over-adjust, creating more risk for themselves.

Remember that with any trade, adjustments are not designed to turn a losing trade into a winner. Instead, they are meant to create a new trade with different risk parameters. There is no magic formula that will allow you to win every trade.

Scenario #1- If There Are Significant Price Movements Early and You Don't Have a Stop Loss

If you enter a trade and it looks like a loser from the outset, check if your market outlook has changed from your initial assumptions. If yes, your best bet is to buy back the entire Iron Butterfly. By doing this, you may be able to exit the trade for less than your max loss. You'll be marking this trade as a loss, and with a long way to expiry, so it's essential that you only do this if you are certain your initial hypothesis was wrong. If the price has little chance of reversing within your profit boundaries, then carry out this adjustment.

Scenario #2 - If There Are Significant Price Movements Closer to Expiry and You Don't Have a Stop Loss

Let's say you enter a trade with 45 days to expiry, and with 12 days left, the price of the underlying blows through the short strike on the call portion of the trade. Now your long put is far OTM and thus has little value. In this scenario, we can move our long put option closer to the short, to create a new profile, which is still a net credit and maintains little risk on the untested side.

Note that this strategy will only work if the new option's price is low enough that you can still maintain a net credit on the trade. If prices are high and you eat into a significant portion of your initial profits, you're now left with a lopsided trade in terms of risk/reward ratio. Let's look at this using an example.

Let's say we sell a $10 wide iron butterfly on Papa John's (NASDAQ:PZZA), which is currently trading at $99.50, for a net credit of $5.50. Our 10 point wide butterfly would consist of these legs:

- Buy $89 put
- Sell $99 put
- Sell $99 call
- Buy $109 call

Our net credit on the trade is $5.50. If the stock rallies to 115, we may have the opportunity to sell the 89 strike and purchase another put at a 94 strike for a net debit of $0.30. This means our net credit is now $5.20, but we have just a five dollar wide put spread component of the Butterfly (because our short strike remains at 99.)

We now have no risk to the downside, since the stock price could drop below 89 and our put spread would be worth $5.00 at expiration, but we've collected $5.20 and would make $0.20 overall.

As you can see here, this adjustment strategy only works if we can buy the 94 strike for less than $0.50. If it is more than $0.50, oour trade will still lose if it falls below 89.

Scenario #3 - Doing Nothing as a Trade Management Strategy

This sounds counterintuitive, but doing nothing is a legitimate management strategy for Butterflies. This is because they're a defined risk trade where you know your max profit and max loss up front. Instead of focusing on the best adjustment strategies, it would be better to focus on your entry points and the data you had available, which caused you to choose those entry points. In our experience working with people new to iron butterflies, the problem tends to be with their entry points rather than their trade management.

AVOIDING THE WORST CASE SCENARIO FOR CREDIT SPREADS

As we stated earlier, the most important factor in successful options trading is risk management. The following example is an incredibly rare trading event, where a trader was assigned an option after expiration. This resulted in massive losses for him. We'll explain how it happened, plus what you can do to ensure it never happens to you.

We should stress that the trader himself was not at fault here. He fell victim to a little known quirk of options trading, combined with his broker's poor communication.

We'll start with the basics. How is it possible a trader was assigned an option after expiration? Below is an excerpt of the rule from the Option Industry Council's website (Options Exercise, 2020):

> *Can I exercise my right to buy the stock at any time up to the expiration date?*
>
> *As the holder of an equity or ETF call option, you can exercise your right to buy the stock throughout the life of the option up to your brokerage firm's exercise cut-off time on the last trading day.* ***Options exchanges have a cut-off time of 4:30 p.m. CST, for receiving an exercise notice.*** *Be aware that most brokerage firms have an earlier cut-off time for submitting exercise instructions in order to meet exchange deadlines.*

We've highlighted the most important sentence in bold. The stock market closes at 3PM Central Time (4PM EST), but options can be exercised up to 90 minutes *after* this time. Therefore, if your stock experiences significant after-hours movement, it can mean that an option that you thought had expired OTM, might move ITM during this 90-minute period. Which puts you at risk of being assigned.

Here was the trade in question. The trader sold five contracts of the 410/409 put spreads on Tesla. Therefore his max loss was $500 ($1 wide spread * five contracts.) At market close (3PM CST), Tesla was trading at $418. That means the trader's put spreads were out of the money and would expire worthless.

However, at 4:16PM CST, Tesla had fallen to $393, sending his $410 short put ITM. The trader was assigned all five contracts. This meant he was forced to purchase 500 shares of Tesla at $410, which represents a position of $205,000.

At this point, the trader was not in any real danger, because he could still exercise his $409 long puts to cancel the losses from the $410 puts. Or so he thought…

However, his broker did not inform him of the $410 put exercise until well after the 4:30PM CST cutoff time. This meant he could not exercise his $409 put, and it expired worthless. He was left with an order of 500 shares of Tesla, which approximated to a cash position of $205,000. As his account was only worth around $30,000, his broker liquidated the position for a $30,000 loss.

Ensuring This Never Happens to You

What transpired above was a series of unfortunate events, but ones that were entirely within the boundaries of options trading. The trader in question was an experienced options trader, who had initially placed a very conservative trade. The result was a combination of a quirk in options trading rules, and poor communication from the trader's brokerage firm.

The easiest way to mitigate this risk is to close any short options a couple days before expiration, even if they aren't ITM. You'll make a slightly lower profit on each trade, but it will give you peace of mind knowing that you won't put your entire account in jeopardy if a catastrophic scenario occurs. If you take max profit at 75% like stated earlier in this chapter, you're at less risk of this scenario occurring, but you should still close out your trades a couple of days before expiration to ensure it doesn't happen.

FREEMAN CREDIT SPREAD RULE #13

TO AVOID BEING ASSIGNED AFTER HOURS, CLOSE YOUR TRADE 1-2 DAYS BEFORE EXPIRY

For a full, in-depth explanation of this exact scenario occurring with the trade in question, please watch the full video at:
http://freemanpublications.com/creditspread30k

Note: Since this incident occurred, it has come to our attention that this scenario has affected multiple people, most notably those using the Robinhood platform. It turns out Robinhood did not alert traders until eight hours after the market had closed. For this reason, as well as ones we stated earlier in the book, we do not recommend using Robinhood to trade options of any kind.

You can also call your broker to see what their rules are for a scenario like this. For example, the Thinkorswim platform states they will automatically exercise your protective put in this case, mitigating your risk. Always call your broker to confirm this and make sure you get any answers in written format via email if you need to refer back to them later.

MONEY MANAGEMENT

Money management is essential when it comes to trading. Unlike passive long-term investing, you'll be moving in and out of the markets far more regularly. You won't be establishing as many positions as a day trader would but assuming you stick to the 30 to 45-day window we recommend, you'll likely have at least one active trade open per month.

A common question that many people ask when viewing a strategy is: How much money can I make from this? The answer is that it depends on how much you risk per trade. It's possible to earn 200% per year, and it's equally possible to earn 5%.

As we've mentioned in our other books, you need to move past thinking in terms of absolute returns and focus on risk-adjusted returns instead. There are many risk-adjusted metrics that professionals use.

You can track basic risk-adjusted metrics such as the Sharpe ratio or the Sortino ratio to measure account performance. However, when it comes to successful credit spread trading, you need to begin with the amount of money you risk per trade and focus on that solely.

If you follow our previous recommendations regarding profit taking and loss levels. You won't have to worry too much about the underlying math in your trades working out in your favor. This means your biggest consideration in how much to risk per trade, is the size of your account, and the price of the option spreads. This is because you need that much cash or margin in your account for the trade to go through.

For a credit spread, the margin requirement for each spread (with most/major brokerages) is calculated as:

(Spread Width - Credit Received) x 100

If you sell a $12 wide spread for $3.22, the margin requirement would be (($12 - $3.22) x 100) = $878 in margin requirement per spread sold, as the maximum loss potential per spread would be $878.

If you're starting out, we recommend risking no more than 10% of your account per trade. If you're from the world of directional trading, this will sound like a ridiculously high number. Indeed, most directional traders should not risk more than 0.5% of their account. However, with options, we can get away with risking this much for two reasons.

First, we're implementing net credit spread strategies that have a high success rate. We're also assuming that you will paper trade strategies before jumping into the live market. This means you'll be well-versed with your strategies and won't be assuming undue risk. The second reason for a 10% per trade risk rate is that you'll be placing one to two trades per month.

We advise against placing more than one trade or trading more than one instrument as you'll shortly learn. If you're trading a low number of instruments, your per-trade risk can be much higher. Also, remember that you'll be taking your losses as a function of your credit earned, not at the max loss number. All of this means a 10% risk number is perfectly fine.

ACCOUNTS AND OTHER TIPS

Money and risk management go hand in hand, and the biggest rule to observe when trading options is that you need to separate your options trading account from your long-term investing account. Your long-term investment account has nothing to do with your trading strategies. This will allow you to remain invested no matter what, and you won't end up selling your long-term stock holdings to cover option assignments.

Selling at the wrong time is one of the biggest reasons individual investors don't make money in the markets. Driven by panic or by euphoria, they often sell at the worst moment possible and end up losing the power of compounding. To make a lot of money, you need to remain invested for long periods and keep contributing to your account regularly. This is not how money is made in trading. Hence, keep your accounts separate.

Now that you know how your account needs to be set up and how much you'll risk per trade, the question of how much you can expect to earn is easier to answer. Assuming you follow the rules we've previously outlined, you'll earn between 1-3% percent per month. This isn't the 20,000% gain that some Twitter traders like to post screenshots of. However, from an asset investment perspective, this is a fantastic return. Best of all, it's fully scalable. Many trading strategies make large returns when the capital invested is small, but they fall apart when larger sums are involved. With credit spreads, it's true that you can't expect to run them efficiently if you have billions of dollars. However, you'll probably be very happy with a trading account that is one percent of that. We can confidently say that even if you have millions in your trading account, you'll be able to generate these kinds of returns safely.

As your account size grows, it's best to dial down the risk you run with every trade until you reach a more conventional two percent. This is because you will have less of your account at risk and you'll still be able to earn a good amount of money from your trades. If your account is small, you'll probably need to risk 10% as we mentioned earlier.

What if your account is so small that even a 10% per trade risk doesn't cover most stocks' margin requirements? In such cases, you have two choices. The first is to choose lower width spreads and stick to trading them at all times. The second is to accumulate enough capital until you have enough to risk 10% per trade successfully. Set aside some money regularly every month until you have enough to meet this risk limit.

We do not advise risking more than this to trade options. This will create massive fluctuations in your account as your trade progresses and might result in you closing your trades out too early due to the fear of losing money. Stay patient and accumulate money until you have enough to trade properly.

Instruments To Trade

How many instruments should you trade? This is a tough question to answer for most traders. It depends on how much you're risking per trade. As a rule of thumb, you don't want your risk to exceed 10% per month. However, if you place five positions, you'll be risking 50% or half of your account. This isn't a good way to trade.

Therefore, the best thing to do is to limit your monthly risk to 10%. Since all of your trades will be within the 30 to 45-day period, a per trade risk of 10% means you'll have just one position active during the month. If you risk 5% per trade, you can open two positions and so on. This gives you a good way to limit your risk and tie it to your per trade risk.

When choosing instruments, it's best to begin paper trading them before going live. Every instrument has different sets of traders active in them, and it will take you some time to adjust to its rhythms. Observe your chosen instruments for at least two months before committing to trade them live. It's best if you observe them for at least six months or two quarters. This will give you an idea of how volatility changes around earnings season.

Realistically speaking, you will need to master moves in two stocks at the very least. Preferably, their earnings season will be spaced apart so that they're in different months. This way you'll always have one instrument to operate in. Do you need more than two instruments? Some traders prefer to add more as they grow, but our opinion is that two is more than enough.

In trading, it's better to go deeper rather than wide. This means if you master trading a few stocks, you'll make more than enough money. Don't get carried away or get influenced by images of traders sitting in front of 10 screens. Many successful traders visit their trading platforms once a day, trade one or two instruments, use simple strategies, and make a ton of money.

Master a few instruments instead of the entire S&P 500 and you'll make a lot of money. Do not confuse complexity for competence. Some of the worst traders are those who sit themselves down in front of multiple screens and try to make sense of far too many instruments. This is true of active traders. The strategies we've outlined in this book aren't active ones or as active as the ones that most directional traders implement. There's no reason for you to become wedded to your laptop. Specialization is the key to large profits, so make this your goal.

14

THE LONG-TERM PROFIT MINDSET

"If investing is entertaining, if you're having fun, you're probably not making any money. Good investing is boring."

— GEORGE SOROS

I f we had to summarize trading into one word, we'd say "boring." That doesn't mean you won't enjoy it or that you shouldn't be passionate about it. We're trying to say that excitement in the context of the markets is a bad thing. Traders are mostly focused on the short-term prices of stocks, and in the short term, most movements are created by emotions.

Euphoria, greed, fear and excitement create more moves in the market than are strictly necessary. If your trading or investing feels like a rollercoaster, you're doing it wrong. We're not saying you should be bored to the point of dozing off in your chair when you trade. Instead, the ideal mood is one of engaged boredom. Think of it as watching a TV show you're mildly interested in. This is irrespective of whether or not you have a position in the market.

Many traders get extremely excited when they have a position because their money is now at risk. Excitement can go two ways. It can prompt extreme happiness, or it can promote extreme sadness and anxiety. This is no way to trade. Thankfully, with credit spreads you capture your entire profit upfront, and there's not much else you need to do after that. This goes a long way towards removing any source of "excitement" you might feel.

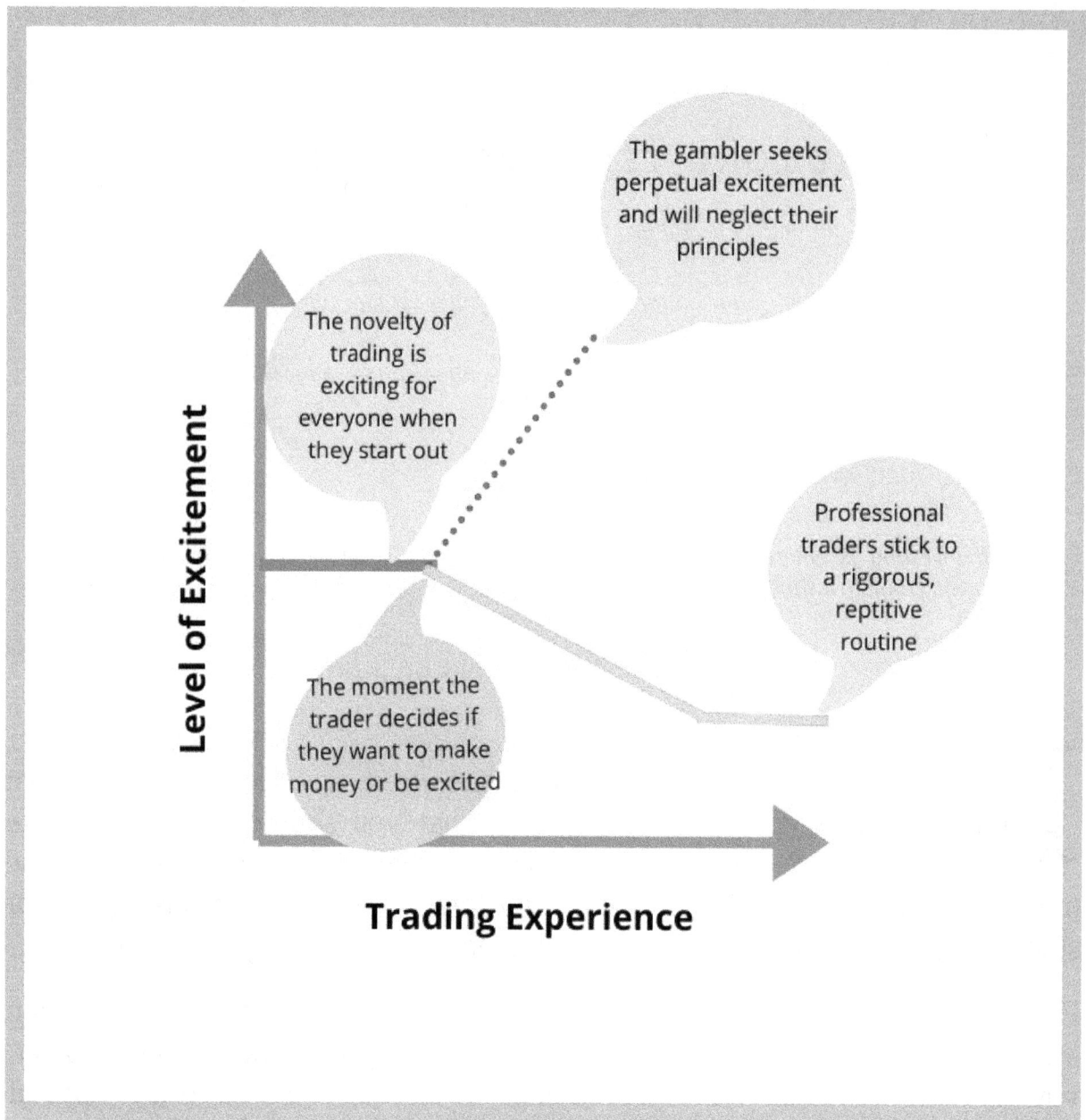

Figure 20: The above excitement vs. boredom concept visualized

To maintain as much consistency as possible, your trading routine should be geared towards minimizing as many unexpected occurrences. Let's look at how you can set this up.

THE IDEAL TRADING ROUTINE

Many elements go into your routine. First let's deal with your actions during the trading day. The markets open at 9:30AM EST, and between 9:30AM and 11AM is where the majority of trading volumes occur. You don't need to be present on the spot to place orders quickly. As we covered earlier, you'll be trading high liquidity instruments, and this means you can theoretically place orders throughout the day without any adverse consequences.

However, we advise placing your orders during the initial period because price spreads tend to contract during this time. Stay away from the opening bell since this is when overnight orders come rushing in, and volatility will be high. Let the market settle, and then enter your trades. This means you don't need to witness the opening bell. Instead, make sure your trades are placed by 11AM and leave it at that.

Once your trades are placed, there's nothing else you need to do during the day. In subsequent days, you'll monitor your position throughout the day by checking in to see its unrealized profit or loss and make adjustments according to the rule-based strategies we've already outlined. Don't get carried away and hang around in your trading platform too much since this might tempt you to place more trades.

If you've struggled with this in the past, simply log out and go do something else. Most readers of this book will have full-time jobs, so it's best to focus on that instead of remaining glued to your trading screen. Once the markets close, after-hours trading begins. You can place your orders during these times if you missed the market hours, provided you can still find a good spread. However, it's best not to make a habit of it. After-hours trading is when spreads notoriously widen. Also, if you're entering a limit order, your broker might not be able to fill your order. In fact, most brokers won't allow you to place limit orders after hours.

During market hours or when you're placing orders, stay away from social media. In fact, stay away from social media at all times unless you can practice a good deal of self-control. Following people on Twitter for trade recommendations is not a sustainable way of making money. Remember, you need just one or two trades every month. If you're trading just two instruments or even five, there's no need for you to scour the internet for more trade ideas.

Feel free to watch YouTube videos on options trading after the market is closed. Don't do so if you're entering orders or are analyzing possible trade setups. Avoid any distractions when you're placing your orders. If you find yourself in front of the trading screen for the majority of the day, either focus on it completely or walk away.

Diet, Exercise and Sleep

These three factors will do a lot more to affect your trading than any technical analysis indicator. You cannot trade well if you aren't taking care of yourself by eating good food, sleeping well and exercising enough. Let's begin with your diet. This isn't a fitness book, so we're not going to debate the advantages of the keto diet over the paleo diet and so on. Eat whatever you want, but make sure it reduces inflammation in your gut or keeps it to a minimum. Your gut and brain are linked, and research has proven this many times over (Robertson, 2018). Avoid processed food as much as possible and stick to whole food sources.

If your stomach is upset, your brain is less likely to focus, and you're going to make poor decisions. Exercise is linked directly to your appetite. Whatever your choice of staying active is, it's important that you engage in it at least four times every week. If you're someone who hasn't been active for a long time, focus on breaking a sweat at least once a week.

It doesn't matter what your chosen activity is. Make sure you're engaging in it four times every week and are giving your body a good workout. If you're completely inactive right now, start by taking a brisk walk and build from there.

Proper diet and exercise will help you sleep better. Sleep is an essential part of a healthy lifestyle. The easiest way to ruin your mood is not to sleep enough. Make sure your bedroom is dark and quiet. Keep the temperature at optimal levels, and get at least six to seven hours of sleep per night.

Hydrate yourself throughout the day. Make sure you drink your 8 glasses of water every day. Drinking enough water ensures you'll remain healthy more than taking any medicines. Also, minimize alcohol intake since this dehydrates your body. You don't have to eliminate it if you don't want to, but certainly, minimize intake prior to trading days.

Mental Health

In the post-COVID world, our workspaces have become increasingly isolated. Full-time traders are used to this since trading is a solitary activity. However, regular workplaces have also become remote these days, and mental health is a huge issue. Monitoring your mental health is crucial if you want to make good trades. Trading requires you to make a number of discretionary decisions, and making good ones is impossible if your mental health isn't optimal.

Consider joining a trading community so you can surround yourself with like-minded people. No one will understand your predicament like other traders, and sometimes it's fun just to talk shop. The other benefit of being around people with similar interests and goals is that you avoid the negative talk that society at large has about trading and the financial world.

If you're looking for a community of like-minded people, join our Facebook Group at

https://freemanpublications.com/facebook

Another fantastic tool that is universally beneficial is meditation. Meditation helps calm down your body and mind, and it acts as a tool to separate yourself from your results. This sounds nuanced, but being able to differentiate between "I made a bad trade" and "I'm a bad trader" is of the utmost importance. You can find many free meditation tutorials on YouTube as well as paid apps like Headspace and Stop.Breathe.Think.

Whatever you do, never trade under the following conditions:

- Hungry
- Angry
- Lonely
- Tired
- Under the influence of drugs or alcohol

Avoiding these conditions will put you in a good position to trade. Establish a consistent routine and repeat it over and over. That's all there is to trading successfully.

CONCLUSION

Successful credit spread trading is like building a house. You begin by laying the foundations and then build on top of it brick by brick. You'll need to keep building on the gains you've previously made and keep educating yourself. Don't make the mistake of choosing short-term gains for long-term success. You might get frustrated in the short term, but remember that delayed gratification is the key to long-term success.

As we reach the end of this book, we'd like to remind you of the importance of generating income from your portfolio, as opposed to just capital gains. Capital gains are great, but in a low interest world it's important to generate income that can bring you additional cash flow. With savings accounts and other typical modes of passive investment unprofitable, you need to implement net credit spreads and other income generating strategies into your trading routine.

Credit spreads can bring you an average of 1-3% every month. If your capital is $5,000, this amounts to $100 per month or $1,200 per year. This doesn't sound like a lot of money, but remember that credit spreads are scalable. You'll earn this income whether your capital is $5,000 or $500,000. In 10 years time, assuming you reinvest your profits and keep earning the same rate of returns, your account balance will grow to $53,825. At that stage you'll be earning an extra $1,100 per month.

Even if you pull out your initial $5,000 after a few years, so you can essentially play with house money, and still be earning a steady 4 figures per month if you stay consistent over a period of multiple years.

And remember, you don't have to be a financial wizard or have a master's degree in statistics when starting out. Here are 3 examples of ordinary people using credit spreads to supplement their income.

"My worst year, I had 29 wins and 4 losses, which comes out to 86.2% winning trades. My best year was last year, 28 wins, 1-loss, 95.6%. The years in between I never got less than 92% wins, so it's just been wonderful." – **Bob M., Florida**

"Trading is going well. I'm currently trading just spreads each month. That'll be three months in a row with an average profit of about $1,500 per month." – **Matt I., Indiana**

"I have been investing in Credit Spreads since August. I pick them based on my own analysis so that I have one spread potentially expiring every week, and I'm looking to earn $250-$1,000 per spread. Results: 51 Trades, 47 Winners (92%), $28,430 in profits after commission (about $557 average per trade)" – **Anthony M.**

Remember to keep things simple when starting out. One of the beauties of credit spreads is that you don't need to use 15 or 20 different technical indicators to set them up. Nor do you need to spend multiple hours monitoring your positions every day.

All you need to trade well are support and resistance levels, Bollinger Bands, and moving averages. These sound ridiculously simple, but that's all you truly need to figure out what the markets are doing.

To cement this principle, consider writing down the quote below in your trading journal:

"I fear not the man who has practiced 10,000 kicks once. I fear the man who has practiced one kick 10,000 times"

— BRUCE LEE

Your trading routine is important, and instead of tailoring it to produce as much excitement as possible, focus on generating consistency. Do the same things over and over as long as they're producing profits for you. If you're finding yourself getting stressed or feeling burnt-out when thinking of your trading, you're probably risking too much money.

We recommend sticking to a maximum limit of 10% per trade. As your account grows, we recommend scaling this back down to 2%. Your priority should always be to maintain your capital, first and foremost. Too many market participants focus on making money and take undue risk. Focus on keeping the money you have and the gains will take care of themselves.

Lastly, keep educating yourself. There are always simpler ways to make money from the markets. Maintain your focus on mastering the process of trading instead of looking at the gains you can potentially make. As we said earlier, focus on eliminating risks and your rewards will take care of themselves. We're positive that this book will help you generate steady income from your portfolio. We wish you the best of luck in your trading!

One final word from us. If this book has helped you in any way, we'd appreciate it if you left a review on Amazon. Reviews are the lifeblood of our business. We read every single one and incorporate your feedback into our future book projects.

To leave an Amazon review, go to:
https://freemanpublications.com/leaveareview

"THE MOST SUCCESSFUL PEOPLE IN LIFE ARE THE ONES
WHO ASK QUESTIONS. THEY'RE ALWAYS LEARNING.
THEY'RE ALWAYS GROWING. THEY'RE ALWAYS PUSHING."

- Robert Kiyosaki

REFERENCES

Bond Algos Tap into ETF Liquidity and Efficiency Gains. (2019, March 18). Finextra Research. https://www.finextra.com/blogposting/16827/bond-algos-tap-into-etf-liquidity-and-efficiency-gains

Frazier, K. C. (2015). *The Process Behind New Medicines.* http://phrma-docs.phrma.org/sites/default/files/pdf/rd_brochure_022307.pdf

Lewis, M. (2015). *Flash boys : a Wall Street revolt.* W.W. Norton & Company.

Options Exercise. (2020). Optionseducation.Org. https://www.optionseducation.org/referencelibrary/faq/options-exercise

projectoption. (2020). Options Trading With Credit Spreads (FULL Trading Plan w/ Results) [YouTube Video]. In *YouTube.* https://www.youtube.com/watch?v=XBxDtcPu3PA

Robertson, R. (2018, June 27). *The Gut-Brain Connection: How it Works and The Role of Nutrition.* Healthline. https://www.healthline.com/nutrition/gut-brain-connection#:~:text=The%20Bottom%20Line&text=Millions%20of%20nerve

www.ingramcontent.com/pod-product-compliance
Lightning Source LLC
Chambersburg PA
CBHW081819200326
41597CB00023B/4313